RELIGION, LAW AND THE ROLE OF FORCE

A Study of Their Influence on Conflict and on Conflict Resolution

Based on a seminar sponsored by the Tanenbaum Center for Interreligious Understanding and held in cooperation with Princeton University

Compiled and Edited by
J.I. Coffey and Charles T. Mathewes

Transnational Publishers

Published and distributed by Transnational Publishers, Inc.
Ardsley Park
Science and Technology Center
410 Saw Mill River Road
Ardsley, NY 10502

Phone: 914-693-5100
Fax: 914-693-4430
E-mail: info@transnationalpubs.com
Web: www.transnationalpubs.com

Library of Congress Cataloging-in-Publication Data

Religion, law, and the role of force : a study of their influence on conflict and on conflict resolution / compiled and edited by J.I. Coffey and Charles T. Mathewes.

p. cm.

"Based on a seminar sponsored by the Tanenbaum Center for Interreligious Understanding and in cooperation with Princeton University."

Includes bibliographical references and index.

ISBN 1-57105-263-1 — ISBN 1-57105-280-1 (pbk.)

1. Religion and law. 2. Conflict management—Religious aspects. I. Coffey, Joseph I. II. Mathewes, Charles T., 1969– III. Tanenbaum Center for Interreligious Understanding.

BL65.L.33 R447 2002
261.8'73—dc21 2002029116

Manufactured in the United States of America

CONTENTS

ACKNOWLEDGEMENTS

This book, even more than most, is the work of many hands, many minds and many hearts, for without the enthusiastic support of some who played no direct role in its shaping it would never have came into being. First among these is Georgette F. Bennett, Ph.D., President of the Tanenbaum Center for Interreligious Understanding, under whose auspices the study which led to this manuscript was conceived and conducted; without her unflagging support and personal effort we would never have had the resources required for the effort. And backing her—and us—through their contributions to the Tanenbaum Center were the FJC (Foundation for the Jewish Community) and Paul Newman, at the suggestion of Leo Nevas.

Nor were these the only individuals who provided support. At Princeton University, we received donations from:

- The Center for the Study of Religion (Professor Robert Wuthnow, Director.)
- The Center of International Studies (Professor Aaron Friedberg, Director.)
- The Council of the Regional Studies (Professor Jeffrey Herbst, Director.)
- The Lichtenstein Institute for the Study of Self-Determination (Professor Wolfgang Danspeckgruber, Director.)

And this was in addition to both the administrative support and the intellectual stimulus provided by others at the University.

Foremost among these was Richard A. Falk, Albert G. Milbank Professor of International Law and Practice, Princeton University, who served as a member of our Steering Committee. In this he was joined by Dr. Jane Holl-Lute, Executive Vice President of the United Nations Foundation, former Executive Director of the Carnegie Commission on Preventing Deadly Conflict; and Dr. James Turner Johnson, Professor of Religion at Rutgers University, who capped his intellectual involvement by contributing a paper on *The Law of Nations: Religion, Ethics and International Law Bearing on Conflict and Peace.*

Of him, as of all the contributors, it must be said that he combined great and relevant knowledge with intellectual rigor, analytical skills and an ability to write clearly which you will find manifested in the papers that follow. Equally importantly, from the viewpoint of the editors, they showed a willingness to adjust both the content and the context of their inputs so that these would mesh more smoothly with one another and fit better into the overall framework of the book. For this alone, they should all be blessed!

We would also like to note the stellar performance of Ms. Nahide Bayrasli, Program Associate in the Program on Religion and Conflict Resolution at the Tanenbaum Center. Ms. Bayrasli played a significant role in everything from organizing the conference at Princeton University at which both authors and guests discussed *Religion, Law and the Role of Force* to helping to bring the resultant product into a coherent whole to preparing the manuscript for publication. And in this process, her substantive contributions were even more notable than her administrative ones.

Finally, we, the editors, would like to thank Mr. John Berger of Transnational Publishers, Inc. both for accepting for publication what was at the time an intellectual skeleton and for helping us, by his comments and suggestions, not only to flesh it out but to beautify it. We hope that the resultant product is both appealing and solid.

J. I. Coffey, Ph.D.
Director Emeritus
Program on Religion and
Conflict Resolution
Tanenbaum Center for
Interreligious Understanding

Charles T. Mathewes, Ph.D.
Professor of Religion
University of Virginia

CONTRIBUTORS

Dr. Joseph I. Coffey, Co-Editor, Director Emeritus, Program on Religion and Conflict Resolution, Tanenbaum Center for Interreligious Understanding. He is Distinguished Service Professor Emeritus of Public and International Affairs, University of Pittsburgh. He has also taught at Carnegie Mellon University, at Georgetown and at West Point. During his Army career, he served in the Intelligence Directorate, in the Plans Division, in the Office of the Assistant Secretary of Defense (ISA) and on the White House Staff. Following retirement, he became a consultant to ACDA, AID, USIA, the Department of Defense and the State Department. He also directed research programs at the Institute for Defense Analyses, at the Bendix Aerospace Systems Division and at the University of Pittsburgh.

Dr. Coffey has authored or co-authored thirteen books and monographs and has published more than forty articles on strategy, deterrence, arms control and security policy. He has traveled extensively in Eastern and Western Europe, where he carried out research, conducted interviews and lectured at universities, at military schools and to civilian groups.

Ambassador James E. Goodby, Senior Fellow, The Brookings Institute. He is a career Foreign Service Officer, with broad experience in national security affairs and its subset: arms control. He has held appointments not only in the State Department in Washington, but in US Missions overseas, as well as on the NATO Staff and on the NSC Staff. He has been posted as Ambassador to Finland, as Chairman of the US Delegation to the Organization for Security and Cooperation in Europe and as the head of the US Mission negotiating for the redirection of nuclear arms and fissionable materials in Russia, Ukraine and Kazakhstan. He has had academic appointments at Carnegie-Mellon University, Stanford and elsewhere and has held research positions at the Brookings Institute and at USIP, where he was a William Jennings Fellow. He is the author of a major book on the future of Russia and of numerous articles and monographs on arms control, on European security and on peacemaking.

General Andrew J. Goodpaster, Chairman Emeritus and Senior Fellow, The Eisenhower World Affairs Institute. He was Staff Secretary and Defense Liaison Officer to President Eisenhower from 1954 until 1961. He also served at Supreme Headquarters Allied Powers Europe; as Commander of a US Division in Germany; Assistant to the Chairman, Joint Chiefs of Staff; Director of the Joint Staff; Commandant of the National War College; Deputy

Commander of US Forces in Vietnam; Commander-in-Chief, United States European Command and Supreme Allied Commander, Europe. He assisted President Nixon in organizing his administration for the conduct of foreign policy and international security affairs. Gen. Goodpaster has been awarded the US Medal of Freedom as well as military decorations including the DSC; the Defense DSM with Oak Leaf Cluster; the Army DSM with 3 Oak Leaf Clusters; the Silver Star; the Purple Heart with Oak Leaf Clusters; and others.

Rabbi Dr. Marc Gopin, Adjunct Professor, Fletcher School of Law and Diplomacy. Some of his recent publications include: *Between Eden and Armageddon: The Future of Religion, Violence and Peacemaking* (2000); "Between War and Peace in Judaism and Islam," Festschrift in Memory of Dr. Marvin Fox (forthcoming); "Mennonite Conflict Resolution Practice," *From the Ground Up: Mennonite Contributions to International Peacebuilding* (2000). He is Senior Associate in the Program for Preventative Diplomacy, Center for Strategic and International Studies (1996–present) and consultant to the International Conflict Resolution Program at Columbia University, the Tanenbaum Center's Program on Religion and Conflict Resolution, the World Bank, and the Israeli Embassy. Dr. Gopin is also a senior level negotiator in the Palestinian/Israeli peace process, on religious and cultural factors of the conflict.

Dr. James T. Johnson, Professor of Religion and Associate Member of the Graduate Department of Political Science, Rutgers University. His research and teaching have focused principally on the historical development and application of moral traditions related to war, peace, and the practice of statecraft. His books include *Ideology, Reason, and the Limitation of War* (Princeton, 1975); *Just War Tradition and the Restraint of War* (Princeton, 1981); *Can Modern War be Just?* (Yale, 1984); *The Quest for Peace: Three Moral Traditions in Western Cultural History* (Princeton, 1987); *The Holy War Idea in Western and Islamic Traditions* (Penn State, 1997); *Moral Issues in Contemporary War* (Yale, 1999); and *Just War and Jihad: Historical and Theoretical Perspectives on War and Peace in Western and Islamic Traditions* (Greenwood, 1991). He is also a Trustee, Editorial Board member, and former General Editor of *The Journal of Religious Ethics.*

Dr. David Little, Professor of Religion and Ethnicity, Harvard Divinity School. Prior to his position at Harvard, he was senior scholar in religion, ethics, and human rights at the United States Institute of Peace in Washington, D.C. From 1996 to 1998, he was a member of the U.S. State Department Advisory Committee on Religious Freedom Abroad. He taught previously at Yale Divinity School, Virginia, Brown, and several other colleges and universities. He has written in the areas of moral philosophy, moral theology, history of ethics, and the sociology of religion, with a special interest in comparative ethics, human rights, religious liberty, and ethics and international affairs. He is author with Scott W. Hibbard of *Islamic Activism and U.S. Foreign Policy* and author of two of the volumes in the USIP series on Religion, Nationalism, and Intolerance: *Ukraine—The Legacy of Intolerance and Sri Lanka—The Invention of Enmity*. He is currently working on a study tentatively entitled "Rights and Emergencies: Protecting Human Rights in the Midst of Conflict."

Dr. Charles T. Mathewes, Co-Editor, is Assistant Professor of Religious Studies at the University of Virginia, where he also teaches in the faculty of the Political and Social Thought Program. Dr. Mathewes is also a permanent fellow at the Center for Religion and Democracy. His first book, *Evil and the Augustinian Tradition*, will be published this fall by Cambridge University Press.

Dr. Paul Mojzes, Provost, Academic Dean and Professor of Religious Studies, Rosemont College. He also taught at University of New Hampshire, Lasalle Jr. College, Lycoming College, Florida Southern College, and Villanova University. He was also a professor and dean at the Graz Center, Graz Austria, from 1969–1979. Dr. Mojzes was the co-editor of the *Journal of Ecumenical Studies* and the editor of *Religion in Eastern Europe*. He is the author of five and the editor of several books and has written about 100 articles. He has lectured widely in the US and abroad. His latest books are *Religious Liberty in Eastern Europe and the USSR: Before and After the Great Transformation* (1992) and *Yugoslavia Inferno: Ethnoreligious Warfare in the Balkans* (New York: Continuum, 1994). His most recent book, *The Study of Religion in an Age of Global Dialogue* (Temple University Press, 2000), is co-authored by Leonard Swidler. He is also a member of the Europe Committee of the National Council of Churches.

Dr. Albert C. Pierce, Director, Center for the Study of Professional Military Ethics, USNA. He has been Professor of Military Strategy at the National War College, Washington, D.C., since 1985, and he has taught courses in military strategy, the use of military force, civil-military relations, ethics, national security policy, and national security policymaking. He is also co-director of a National War College-Carnegie Council on Ethics and International Affairs multi-year project on ethical challenges and the future of conflict. Among his publications are "Just War Principles and Economic Sanctions," *Ethics & International Affairs*, Volume 10, 1996; "Crisis Management in the White House and the Pentagon," in Preston Niblack, editor, *Managing Military Operations in Crises* (RAND, 1991); "The Department of Defense and Media Politics," in David C. Kozak and James M. Keagle, editors, *Bureaucratic Politics and National Security* (Lynne Riener Publishers, 198 8); "The Strategic Defense Initiative: European Perspectives," in Catherine M. Kelleher and Gale A Mattox, editors, *Evolving*

European Defense Policies (Lexington Books, 1986); and "Issues Facing the New Administration," in the *AEI Foreign Policy and Defense Review*, published by the American Enterprise Institute in 1981.

Dr. Abdulaziz A. Sachedina, Professor of Religious Studies, University of Virginia. It has been his personal mission in the Muslim community to increase interreligious understanding and cooperation with other faith communities to create a better environment for future generations. His first encounter with interfaith conflict was in India, where he was a student, from 1963–66. As his studies took him to Iran (1966–71) he learned more about the intrafaith conflict that plagues the Muslim community in Pakistan, Lebanon, and Iraq. His commitment to search for this inclusive theology in Iran and Iraq was extended to juridical formulations, which he saw to be the main source of mutual dehumanization in the community and its relationship with the world outside. He also spent four years studying and debating with the ayatollahs in Iran and Iraq to understand underlying messianic elements that were operative in creating "triumphalist" End of Time theology, with its intolerance towards those who did not share that messianic aspiration. Some of his publications include, *Islamic Messianism: The Idea of the Mahdi in Twelver Shi'ism* (State University of New York, Albany, 1980); co-author with David Little and J. E. Kelsay, *Human Rights and the Conflict of Cultures: Western and Islamic Perspectives on Religious Liberty* (U of South Carolina Press, 1998); and *Islamic Roots of Democratic Pluralism* (Oxford UP, 2000).

Dr. Donald Shriver, President Emeritus, Union Theological Seminary. He served as president of UTS until 1991, when he took up fulltime teaching at Union as William E. Dodge Professor of Applied Christianity. He retired as president and professor emeritus in June 1996, having held adjunct teaching appointments at the Jewish Theological Seminary, Drew University, and the schools of Business, Journalism and Law at Columbia University. Dr. Shriver also holds honorary degrees from six colleges and universities. He has been elected as a Berlin Prize Fellow of the American Academy in Berlin for the spring of 1999. His two most recent books are *Beyond Success: Corporations and Their Critics in the Nineties* (with James Kuhn, Oxford 1991) and *An Ethic for Enemies: Forgiveness in Politics* (Oxford, 1995 and 1997).

FOREWORD

On April 21–22, 2001, the Tanenbaum Center for Interreligious Understanding, in cooperation with Princeton University, held a two-day seminar entitled, "Religion, Law and the Role of Force." Gathered at that round table were many of the pioneers who are leading the inquiry into the role of religion in conflict resolution.

The world's major religions are all based on profound notions of justice, peace and good works. But, as the twentieth and all the preceding centuries have shown us, these concepts are terrifyingly easy to subvert. The point was keenly made by United Nations Secretary-General Kofi Annan at a Tanenbaum Center Award Ceremony and Memorial Lecture:

> Religion, sadly, has been misused throughout history in the cause of division, discrimination, and even death. From antiquity through the Crusades to the present day, religion has been distorted, turned from a personal matter of faith and sustenance into a weapon of power and coercion. The cry of the soul for meaning, and for God, has been drowned out by the battle cry of those claiming to have God on their side.

How we can shift religion from being part of the problem to being part of the solution: is the issue that motivates the Tanenbaum Center's programs.

Its mission is to defuse the violence that people do to each other in the name of religion. We are gripped by the conviction that religion can serve as a resource to prevent and resolve deadly conflicts. Religious institutions, religious tenets, religious leaders and other religious actors all bring assets to the table that can be mobilized in dealing with conflict. These may take the form of moral authority, sanctuary, constituencies, communications networks and myriad other resources that range from the theological to the pragmatic.

In recent years, the changing international environment has enhanced the ability of religiously-motivated individuals to influence events and has led to a mounting interest in the helpful role that religion can play in promoting peace and justice. The Tanenbaum Center is committed to exploring what religion can do to achieve these goals and to facilitating efforts to do so. And in so doing, it must grapple with the dilemma of how peacemakers can be true to their own beliefs without demonizing those of others, a move that can only lead to more violence.

One issue of particular interest to us is that of preventing conflict and, should it occur, of alleviating or resolving it. We know that religions differ in how they define the sacred. Those definitions reflect and impact on the cultures in which they arise. Therefore, it is no surprise that religions, religious elements and the state are often in conflict with each other and that the conflict involves force. We must untangle the threads of religion, politics, law and force as a prelude to action. The seminar, whose proceedings appear on these pages, was one attempt to do this and we would like to thank all those who gave time, effort, thought and support to this endeavor.

Georgette F. Bennett, Ph.D.
President
Tanenbaum Center for Interreligious Understanding

PREFACE

The terrorist attacks of September 11, 2001, the first significant assault on mainland America in almost 200 years, had a drastic impact on both public thinking and public policy. For one, they shattered the "myth of invulnerability" that had persisted even during the Cold War, leaving people searching for reassurance. For another, they prompted the government to declare that the Cold War doctrines of deterrence and containment are largely irrelevant and that new threats require new thinking about defense policy. According to President George W. Bush, the gravest danger is that even weak states and small groups could attain a catastrophic power to strike great nations with weapons of mass destruction; assurance that this threat can be blocked will require building up homeland defense, "transforming the military" and adopting a new strategy of striking first at potential attackers.[1]

As Mr. Bush pointed out, these are not the only elements of a revised security policy, which will include gathering broad coalitions to promote peace, preventing the spread of violence and working for a just and peaceful world[2]—aspirations whose achievement will require a truly comprehensive approach to the formulation of that policy. Many factors will enter into that formulation, ranging from definitions of the threat to definitions of justice, from determination of the measures needed to quell terrorism to selection of those required to promote regional security.

We neither can, nor wish to, engage in this process but we do think we have something to contribute to it: an understanding of three important elements that should not be overlooked or scanted by policymakers.

- The first of these is religion. Although commonly viewed as a force for peace, religion can also be an incentive to conflict; in fact, it is identified as such in 15 of the 39 conflicts currently raging in the world.[3] Without understanding the reasons why believers may see war as a preferred option, it may be impossible to understand the cause of a given conflict; without appreciating what religion can and cannot do to ameliorate it, peace may be harder to achieve. And yet, as Douglas Johnston and Cynthia Sampson note in the

---

1 Commencement Address at the United States Military Academy, June 1, 2002, recorded by THE N.Y. TIMES, www.nytimes.com, June 6, 2002, at 3 and 4.

2 *Id.* at 5 and 6.

3 THE DEFENSE MONITOR XXXI, No. 1, 4.

seminal work, *Religion: The Missing Dimension of Statecraft*,[4] under the right circumstances it can be a force for peace.

- In a sense, the same can be said about international law, which is often regarded as an obstacle to desired uses of force rather than as a set of rules that should influence choices among them. True, that law is viewed by many as weak (since its constraints are limited), as ambiguous (since it attempts to reconcile contradictory principles such as state sovereignty and state responsibility) and as inequitable, since it favors strong powers over weak ones. Yet it does provide guidelines for behavior and a basis for reaching judgments about the legality—and consequently the morality—of actions by states, by warring groups and by individuals. And ignoring or circumventing it to obtain transitory advantages may not only slow progress toward a more just and more equitable "law of nations" but may inspire other states to behave in like manner, to the detriment of international security—and that of the United States.
- Finally, we must remember that the use of force is influenced not only by the interests and the policies of those wielding the military instrument but by its internal dynamics. Without an appreciation of those dynamics neither policymakers nor peacemakers are likely to make correct choices; as General Andrew Goodpaster, former Supreme Allied Commander, Europe, said during the conference which preceded this publication, "If war is too important to be entrusted to generals, it is too difficult to be entrusted to amateurs."[5]

This is particularly true since we are concerned not only with the role of force in conflict but with its role in conflict resolution, in bringing about peace when all other instruments of policy have failed to do so. Although this is of general concern, it has special application in intrastate conflicts, since these are widely viewed as posing the greatest threat to international peace and security and as having the greatest likelihood of triggering an interstate conflict.[6] Moreover, such conflicts not only pose

---

[4] RELIGION: THE MISSING DIMENSION OF STATECRAFT, (Johnston, Douglas & Cynthia Sampson, eds., 1995).

[5] Goodpaster, Andrew J. "Religion, Law and the Role of Force: Operational Aspects." P. 8

[6] This opinion was strongly expressed during the Millennium Session of the United Nations; in fact, President Clinton declared that," We find today fewer wars between nations but more wars within them. Such internal conflicts, often driven by ethnic and religious differences, took five million lives in the last decade, most of them completely innocent victims." (Transcript of address at the United Nations, September 6, 2000: N.Y. TIMES, Sept. 7, 2000, A16.) And Mr. Clinton joined representatives of other member states in saying that "the international community must take a side . . . ," a view reflected in the United Nations Millennium Declaration, which stated that "Responsibility for managing . . . threats to inter-

operational problems for the armed forces, they also pose political ones, in that military intervention, even for humanitarian purposes, is widely regarded as a transgression upon the rights of sovereign states and hence as a violation of the Charter of the United Nations. Since Afghanistan, Angola, Sudan, Yugoslavia and other states in which such conflicts have occurred are frequently underdeveloped, underorganized or both, the imposition of "peace" by external forces may not last without the creation of a new and different entity. Thus, Mr. Bush's objective of promoting "moderation and toleration and human rights,"[7] like other efforts to establish a "just peace," may require nation-building on a scale scarcely imagined.

Obviously, this is not an issue with which we can deal in this book—though it is one of which we must remain conscious throughout all our endeavors. What we *will* do is:

- Examine, in Part I, the ways in which religion, law and force work to generate, to curb and to help put an end to armed conflict;
- Focus, in Part II, on their potential impact on the resolution of intra-state conflicts;
- Consider, in Part III, the results of our inquiry, with particular reference to their implications for policies that propose to achieve "peace with justice" through the use of force.

In this way, we hope to focus attention on three of the factors influencing policy choices and policy outcomes in this new and troubled world.

---

national peace and security must be shared among the nations of the world and should be exercised multilaterally"—with the United Nations playing the central role. (*Id.* Sept. 9, 2000, A4.) This does not, of course, rule out interventions by individual nations, either under UN auspices or without them, as evidenced, among other instances by the situation in Congo, where three African states have been fighting in support of the government and three others against it.

7 *Speech at West Point, loc. cit.*, 7.

PART I

RELIGION, LAW AND FORCE: THE EFFECT ON CONFLICT

Force has always been an instrument of policy—as well a means of exacting vengeance, creating terror and seizing booty. Throughout most of history, the only significant obstacle to the use of force was the fear of consequences: victory was never assured, as the fate of Sennacherib's host before the walls of Jerusalem reminds us.

True, adherents of some religions condemned violence in all its forms but others did not and, as we shall see, busied themselves with devising doctrines prescribing when, where and how force should be employed. Nor, until recently were there legal restrictions on the use of force, since the states which made up the international system were both authorized to create armed forces and empowered to employ them; as the inscriptions sometimes found on the breeches of cannon said, these were "Ultima ratio Regis"—"the ultimate argument of the king."

The armed forces themselves suffered few restrictions upon their operations; in fact, until the 19th century the "custom of war" granted soldiers the rights of rape and pillage in a captured city. And even after that changed, constraints mainly covered minor matters such as the treatment of prisoners of war rather than issues such as the nature of military operations.

Over time, this situation began to change. Many who traced the path of history came to believe that it had led only to disaster—a judgment confirmed by the two World Wars of the 20th century—and began to seek alternatives to prior practices. By and large, these individuals argued for the peaceful settlement of disputes, the imposition of limitations on armaments and the establishment of legal barriers to the use of force, many of which have been incorporated into international law. (As Michael Howard put it, we in the modern world have invented peace—and sought to institutionalize it.)[1]

---

1 Howard, Michael. *The Invention of Peace: Reflections on War and International Order.* Yale UP: February 2001.

Furthermore, this endeavor was supported—and in some cases led—by religious elements who saw it as furthering their own objectives of reducing the likelihood and the costs of war. And they have, perhaps surprisingly, been joined by military leaders, who argue that restrictions on the use of force are not only ethical but cost effective. Thus, people of many persuasions have sought to establish a more peaceful world by placing limits on the use of force.

In this section of the book we want to examine the origins of these limits, their nature and, so far as practicable, their effectiveness, before considering, in Section III, what might be done to enhance that effectiveness. And in all three sections we want to consider interactions among religion, law and force and how they impinge on the international environment.

SECTION 1

RELIGION AND CONFLICT

In a very real sense the term "religion" may be misleading: there is not a single religion but hundreds, not a single center of religious power and authority but many—and frequently conflicting—ones. Thus we were forced, *faute de mieux*, to limit our analysis. In this case, we chose to focus on the three Abrahamic faith traditions: Judaism, Christianity and Islam.

There were a number of reasons for this, one being that all three faith traditions have endeavored to formulate rules that should govern the use of force, in contrast to those, such as Baha'i, which have simply condemned it. Another is that their common heritage makes it easier to ascertain and evaluate the principles on the use of force than if we were looking at very disparate religions. A third is that the Christian ethos has permeated the Western world, which is still the most technologically advanced and most powerful segment of the globe and the one exercising the greatest influence on the formulation of international law and the development of codes for the conduct of military operations. And a fourth, it must be said, is because many of today's conflicts involve their adherents, frequently pitted against one another.

In our inquiry we sought answers to four general questions.

- Does the tradition acknowledge "legitimate violence," and if so, for what purposes or objectives?
- How do believers go about deciding on the "just use of force?" Are religious leaders involved in such decisions and if so, how?
- Once war has been started, what constraints, if any, are imposed on the use of force? Do these apply equally to co-religionists and to adherents of other faiths?
- Are these principles and practices changeable? If so, what changes have taken place since their original formulation and how readily can further changes be made?

Before attempting to spell out the limitations that religion may place on the use of force, it is essential to remember two things. The first is that religious traditions are profoundly ambiguous forces, since at one and the same time they convey universalist moral messages that can help to secure peace and promote justice and reflect exclusionist tendencies which can lead to violent and destructive conflict. (As a prelate of the Armenian Apostolic Church said, "Every member of the Church is Armenian; every Armenian is a member of the Armenian Apostolic Church.")[1]

The second is that these traditions are a complex mix of archaism and modernity, so that religious bodies are engaged in on-going debates about how best to stay true to their origins while still meeting the challenges of the present day. In Islam, as Professor Abdulaziz Sachedina points out, the principles governing the occasions when a resort to arms was warranted and the ways in which they should be employed originated in the seventh century Common Era (CE) and crystallized in the ninth, under the Caliphate; obviously, the concept of *jihad* today should take account of the radically different context of the present world. Similarly, the Judaic rules on the use of force, developed more than a thousand years before the Common Era, were designed to deal with the situation of that time and not the present one; moreover, as Marc Gopin[2] points out, Rabbinic Judaism, lacking a sovereign political entity of its own for almost two millennia, was uninterested in further developing theories about the role of force. And even though Christianity has continued to debate and refine the principles governing the use of force devised by Saint Augustine, these were first formulated in the fifth century CE when the Roman Empire spanned the Western World.

As might be expected of guidelines developed under such different circumstances, those of the three Abrahamic faith traditions are very different in nature. For one thing, both Islamic and Judaic law spell out the kinds of wars that are authorized—or prescribed—while Christianity, in "just war" theory, describes a process that should be followed and not a desired outcome. For another, Jewish law does not set rules limiting the conduct of military operations once war has begun, quite the contrary. Islamic guidelines on the use of force differentiate between the treatment of Muslims and of non-Muslims and Christian teaching is, at least in theory, universally applicable. Thus, we would ask our readers, as they peruse the three papers on Religion and Conflict, to be very conscious of their context, as well as of their content.

We would also ask these readers, as they study and assess religious guidelines on the use of force, to bear in mind that:

---

1 Seminar on "Religion and Self-Determination" sponsored by the Lichtenstein Center for the Study of Self-Determination, Princeton University.

2 *See infra* Ch. 1.

- These are specialized codes of conduct governing behavior in time of conflict and may not reflect the larger and more generally applicable guidelines expressed in abjurations such as "And thou shalt love thy neighbor as thyself,"[3] "If two parties among believers fall into a quarrel, make ye peace between them . . ."[4] and "They shall beat their swords into ploughshares. . . ."[5] Indeed, many of the problems in applying religious teachings to the management of conflict reflect the dichotomy between the expressions of love and brotherhood found in all three Abrahamic faith traditions and the specific guidance on the initiation and the conduct of war.
- There is a real question as to whether the efforts to create a more just and more powerful world can be done, and should be done, within the frameworks of the three religions. This is a question which we shall consider not only in the three papers awaiting your eyes but also in other inputs, notably the forthcoming one "The Law of Nations" in Section 2.

---

3 Leviticus 19:18, King James Version.

4 *The Glorious Qur'an*. English translation by A. Yusuf Ali, 1993. Sura 49, verse 9.

5 Issiah 2:4, King James Version.

CHAPTER 1

JUDAISM, THE LIMITS OF WAR, AND CONFLICT RESOLUTION

*Rabbi Dr. Marc Gopin**

INTRODUCTION

The complex nature of the interaction between world religions, peacemaking and conflict generation in recent decades, in addition to the role of religion throughout history, warrants a special area of investigation. The need for this is urgent. Since religion is important to hundreds of millions of people, the political power generated by this commitment will either lead to a more peaceful world or a more violent world, depending on how that power is utilized. Only through understanding the nature of this religious enthusiasm can we hope to steer the religious world in the direction of peacemaking and co-existence. Furthermore, only if peace is, and is perceived to be, a part of a principled and meaningful fulfillment of religious experience, rather than a shady compromise with an unredeemed world, will this commitment take hold in the broadest spectrum of those who are now zealously religious. Methods of peacemaking that continue to focus only on political and intellectual elites, or that fail to address the broadest possible range of religious believers, are leading to systematic and potentially catastrophic diplomatic failures in key areas of the world, such as the Middle East.

This chapter will attempt to tackle these issues from the perspective of Judaism. As a start, it will indicate the limitations of an approach focused largely on the legitimacy or illegitimacy of war, an approach which has dominated traditional Jewish thinking. It will then look at individual religious ethics, which can both expand the range of concerns about justifications for war and provide some guidelines for religiously motivated behavior which can serve to prevent or to ameliorate conflict. And, finally, it will set forth some conclusions about the role of Judaism in conflict and conflict resolution.

* Fletcher School of Law and Diplomacy.

THE LEGITIMACY OF WAR

There are several areas of inquiry regarding peace and war, all of which, for independent reasons, have failed to account for this complex issue. Much of the thinking about peace and conflict in terms of religion has been divided into questions about the legitimacy of war or its conduct. This has a long history, the contours of which have come to be dominated by Christian discussions of "just war" theory or, alternatively, pacifism. There have also been corresponding bodies of literature, going back thousands of years, in other religions on the legitimacy of war and its conduct.[1]

Most of this discussion has a tendency to limit the full range of possible approaches to human problems, religious or otherwise. There is an important and old discussion, for example, about just war in Christianity, especially in Catholicism. There is, however, a far broader Christian discussion over the centuries about interpersonal ethics, human psychology, and the things inside human beings that lead alternatively to love or hate, compassion or rage, peace or conflict. The same is true in numerous other traditions that have a curious split between discussions of war or peace, on the one side, and, on the other, discussions of ethics and psychology, the latter being critical to the capacity, or lack thereof, to create peace. This selective approach to religious literature and experience is the first problem with just war literature.[2]

Moreover, just war literature always focuses on a single, rather limited choice: war or not war. But this is hardly the range of choices that are available to human beings in conflictual situations. One can believe that war is sometimes necessary but also believe that the choice for war, even if it rests on sound moral principles, effectively expresses a com-

---

[1] For a representative sample of essays with accompanying bibliographies, *see* THE ETHICS OF WAR AND PEACE (Terry Nardin ed., 1996).

[2] The same could be said for the secular just war tradition. There is a curious tendency to bifurcate the political and theological calculus of war, and divorce it from the entire range of human ethical arrangements, principles, and intuitions. The latter are critical in preventing wars and ending them, yet are absent from just war discussions. Furthermore, the second subject of just war theory is the proper conduct of war. Here too there is a curious way in which different rules and values apply, as if values that address stealing, dishonor, brutality, have to be seen in some new way during wartime, or even discarded during war. Clearly, advances such as the Geneva Conventions have attempted to place back into war some of the normal, universal considerations of ethics. But just war discussions have a curious way of speaking about major cataclysms in such broad terms that the fate of individual moral decision-making is completely obscured. This may be a bow to military hierarchy and the loss of a soldier's personal choice. But this too has been challenged by recent conventions. Essentially the just war tradition deprives us too much of the range of moral thinking and reflection that are most essential in situations of radical moral complexity, such as a battlefield. An exception to this is Michael Walzer's attempt to investigate the complexity of military choices. *See* MICHAEL WALZER, JUST AND UNJUST WARS (1977).

plete failure of all the other ethical or spiritual directives that are ideally supposed to guide one's actions. It is their absence that leads to conflict and war may now be the only moral course of action possible, assuming one is not a pacifist. For example, these spiritual directives can include a prohibition in both Buddhism and Judaism against selling destructive weapons.[3] The failure to follow this precept leads to violence, and is therefore a critical component in analyzing its genesis according to these spiritual systems of belief and practice. Nevertheless a resulting war may be obligatory due to the obligation of self-defense, at least in Judaism. For example, a complete theological analysis of the Gulf War against Iraq would include a severe condemnation of the Western countries for having armed Saddam Hussein in the first place, with appropriate demands for admission of responsibility and the prevention of such sinful abetting of crime in the future.

Another example might be the directive of boundless love in Christianity, or *metta* in Buddhism, that, were it followed on a day-to-day basis with adversaries, might prevent minor disagreements from turning into violent warfare. In other words, there is a range of ethical practices, spiritual experiences, laws and codes, which inhere in religious life that are virtually left out of just war discussions.[4] The broader ethical literature is the key to serious and constructive approaches to conflict prevention, resolution and reconciliation, in religious societies.

The third problem with just war literature is the lack of consciousness of the variety in cultural context that forms the basis of how people think about conflict, war and peacemaking. There is a tendency to define war and peace in terms of specific religious criteria in only some faith traditions, and almost exclusively in terms of Biblically based religions. But many people the world over are not thinking in terms of Biblically based religions. Even most of those who are rooted in Biblical religion do not in practice make decisions about conflict based on just

---

3 *See* INNER PEACE, WORLD PEACE 129 (Kenneth Kraft ed., 1992). In Judaism the prohibition is on selling weapons to someone who could not be trusted not to commit murder with those weapons, and involves the obligation not to aid someone else to commit a crime. *See* Talmud Bavli (henceforth T.B.) Avodah Zarah 15b; Maimonides *Mishneh Torah*, Laws of Murder 12:12. Of course, the sad truth is that Maimonides' same Laws of Murder also make it obligatory to kill Jewish apostates and heretics wherever this is possible, if they have refused to repent, in addition to a particularly callous attitude to the value of a polytheistic human life. *See id.*, 4:10, 11. Hence, the mixed legacy of the classical sources, although it must be said in fairness to traditional Judaism that Maimonides was particularly harsh as a social legislator on matters of dogma.

4 *See, for example,* John Yoder's argument, in RELIGIOUS PERSPECTIVES ON WAR: CHRISTIAN, MUSLIM, AND JEWISH ATTITUDES TO FORCE AFTER THE GULF WAR 41ff. (David Smock ed., 1992), that a key part of the ethical evaluation of the Gulf War and its conduct should be the question of how Saddam was armed in the first place.

war criteria. Few of them know these criteria at all. Therefore, the entire discussion smacks of elitism and theological speculation—often after the fact—that has little to do with how, when, and why violence is generated by religious people, or why and how peace is sought and cultivated.

This has important ramifications in terms of global relations, as well as domestic relations between disparate cultural groups. The just war concept have been valuable in the attempt to search for global standards of behavior regarding the conduct of war, harking back to their original function in the Middle Ages. It has also been a helpful banner around which to frame opposition to an ugly war. Furthermore, I do not deny the importance of evoking standards, either secular or religious, for shared behavior and values on a universal scale. Conflict prevention will require this ultimately, and certainly the building of civil societies between religious, nonreligious, and multi-religious contexts requires this.

The real problem is that we cannot, while pursuing just war standards, bury cultural specificity or the unique character of all religious expressions when it comes to peace and conflict, without subverting our original intention. These unique qualities must become key to the discussion if we are not simply to repeat the same mistakes of miscommunication across civilizations, or impose standards coercively on others in the name of peace. In particular, it is the broad range of spiritual beliefs and practices that could be useful in creating constructive approaches to preventing conflicts or managing constructive conflicts nonviolently.[5] From the perspective conflict resolution practice, if we consult religious traditions only when war is imminent or on the horizon then we ask their advice only when the real damage has already been done. By the time the sabers are rattling—or the nerve gas is cooking—the great potential of religious interpersonal values to prevent violence has already been emasculated by the violent and terrifying circumstances.

This critique has direct ramifications in terms of humanitarian intervention in the context of choices between war and peace. In the preconflict phase it seems clear that the range of religious values surrounding poverty relief, one of the supreme obligations of both Biblical and rabbinic Judaism, should be operationalized. Relief and development work, especially when done in accordance with the most recent and effective

---

[5] By "constructive conflict" conflict resolution theoreticians are generally alluding to the fact that many conflicts need to occur, and can play a constructive role in creating more just societies or more honest relationships where everyone's needs are openly confronted. Conflict management, in such circumstances, would have as its goal, not the suppression of the conflict but ensuring that conflict does not turn into a destructive (usually meaning violent) enterprise that is self-perpetuating or intractable. With some practice, observers and activists can become fairly adept at distinguishing constructive and destructive conflicts, whether they may be interpersonal, familial or societal. *See* LOUIS KRIESBERG, CONSTRUCTIVE CONFLICTS (1998).

methods, are essential commandments of Judaism. Not only do these ethical strategies of human improvement represent an independent set of righteous religious deeds in Judaism (*mitsvot*), they also are crucial in the pursuit of peace (*redifat shalom*), another important rabbinic commandment.

It is also the case that, even when one has been compelled to use force, according Jewish religious standards, humanitarian intervention may play a critical role in shortening the conflict and minimizing its damaging effects. For example, in the war on terrorism in 2001 it has become clear that pursuing the *al-qaida* terrorist network is crucial for the saving of innocent human lives the world over. We will see later that saving lives (*pikuah nefesh*) is the overriding obligation of Jewish ethics. From a strategic point of view, aggressively pursuing humanitarian intervention in Afghanistan and Pakistan, will be critical to the war effort. Thus, humanitarian intervention will be not only a good and righteous deed, it will also contribute to the overthrow of terrorism and the ultimate salvation of innocent lives.

JEWISH LEGAL RELIGIOUS WAR IN THE CONTEMPORARY CONTEXT

Let us now examine the Jewish legal attitude to warmaking. The matter is subject to extensive debate in the earliest sources. What emerges from that debate is a conception of three types of war: *milhemet hova* (obligatory war), *milhemet mitsvah* and *milhemet reshut* (discretionary war). The first two, for all practical purposes, appear to be the same (at least the way that they have been received in traditional Judaism), namely, a war that is obligatory or considered a *mitsvah*. These wars include the war against the ancient Amalekite nation and the war against the Canaanites and other tribes occupying the land that became Israel. Only these two wars involve the killing of every man, woman and child. Virtually all Talmudic authorities concluded that the war against the Canaanites is finished because they no longer exist. The Amalekite case is different. Some authorities compared them to the Canaanites in the sense that they no longer exist. Others delay the battle with Amalek to the pre-Messianic era.[6]

The latter poses a problem in the sense that, at least according to some

---

6 Reuven Kimelman, *War*, *in* FRONTIERS OF JEWISH THOUGHT 309 (Steven Katz ed., 1992). We have no way to know exactly what motivated each of these rabbis to curtail or eliminate altogether the legal operationalizing of these wars. We do know, however, that this hermeneutic is made in the context of pervasive criticism in Jerusalem by many Jews of both the Hasmoneans and the priestly leadership, especially regarding violence. See M. Eduyot 8:7; E. URBACH, THE SAGES 575–76; 661–65; 995, n.45 (I. Abrahams trans., 1987). But more work needs to be done on the exact connection, if any, between pietistic anti-violence statements, Talmudic legal efforts to circumscribe Jewish war, and the historical context.

authorities, and pervasive in the popular religious Jewish consciousness, is the fact that implacable enemies of the Jewish people truly are in some sense the Amalekites.[7] Nevertheless, it is important to point out that the vast majority of *halakhic* authorities do not consider this kind of war to be operational. This leaves the final kind of obligatory war, which is the war of self-defense. If it is clear that an enemy has attacked a self-governing Jewish entity then it is obligatory to defend oneself. The texts certainly seem to indicate that this obligation is limited to defense in response to attack, *not preemptive strikes*.[8]

Preemptive strikes are a major issue today in the missile age, in the sense that waiting to be attacked could mean waiting to suffer massive losses and even defeat. Thus, there has been considerable discussion in the literature on preemptive strikes, particularly in light of Israel's decisions in 1967 and the questions surrounding the Lebanon war of 1982.[9] The fact is that it remains extremely difficult to justify preemptive strikes as obligatory according to Jewish law, despite the writings of some authorities such as R. Menachem ha-Meiri (d. 1315) who did so, citing several important authorities that specifically defined obligatory war as a response to attack.

This then leaves the category of *milhemet reshut*, discretionary war.

---

7 The fact that once a year it is obligatory in Orthodox Judaism to recite, hear, or read the Biblical verses declaring an eternal war on Amalek has strengthened a continuing sense among some Jews that there will always be people who, when they demonstrate an implacable need to kill Jews, can be considered like Amalek. Furthermore, part of the struggle in Israel today over its future relationship to Arabs and Palestinians, and the territories, involves a minority of religious Jews who actually do consider this period of history to be the pre-messianic period of struggle, which means that war against Amalekites could be operative potentially. Furthermore, every time there is a bombing in which the purpose of the bomb is to kill as many Jews as possible, with no other objective, it confirms in many religious minds that, on a theological plane, Amalek exists and it is the Palestinians, just as it used to be the Nazis.

8 Samuel David Luzzatto indicated that the Biblical text generally cited to justify war can only refer to response to an attack from a group that has made it clear by that attack that they are, in fact, an enemy. *See* HA-MISHTADEL (Vienna, 1847) on Leviticus 20:11, 18.

9 *See* J. David Bleich, *Preemptive War in Jewish Tradition*, (21:1 TRADITION: 3–41 (Spring 1983) and Kimelman, WAR, *supra* note 6. Recent revelations reported about Moshe Dayan's confessions that, pressured by farming interests in the north, he provoked Syria into the 1967 war, in order to make a land grab on the Golan Heights, highlight the trap of theological reflection that is dependent upon limited information from governments, especially when that information is from one side of a conflict. A provocation to acquire farming land would have entirely rewritten the moral and *halakhic* debate about preemptive strikes in 1967. *See Israeli Hero Reveals Hebron Regrets* by Dafna Linzer, ASSOCIATED PRESS (May 11, 1997). There will undoubtedly be debate in the future about Dayan's motivations. Even if it turns out that his land motivations were mixed with security calculations, this would still significantly affect a moral discussion on many war-related *halakhic* issues, such as *pikuah nefesh*, and the decision to risk lives for a military (or agricultural) purpose.

Here we have an interesting set of disagreements. Jacob David Bleich summarizes the traditional attitude to discretionary war by stating quite clearly that it is precluded in modern times, and in fact has been precluded since at least the end of the second Jewish Commonwealth (70 CE), if not earlier. Discretionary war requires a Jewish king, presumably of Davidic descent, a Sanhedrin (ancient Jewish high court), and the *urim ve-tumim* (a breastplate worn by the High Priest, consulted to give its miraculous indication of whether or not to wage war). All three of these institutions have been assumed to be impossible to recreate before the coming of the Messiah, according to traditional Judaism. This point of view is typical of ultra-orthodox Judaism in modern times that has been quite reluctant to follow the lead of Religious Zionism in terms of reconstituting Jewish institutions of power before the Messiah arrives. This represents a subtle but deep fissure regarding Jewish use of state force.

Reuven Kimelman has done extensive work on the parameters of Jewish warfare. He cites the idea, based on precedents in Maimonides, among others, that the Sanhedrin requirement is meant to act as an expression of the needs of the people, and to be a counter-balance to the needs of the sovereign. Furthermore, the former would be in a position to evaluate the rights and wrongs of going to war and conducting it in an *halakhic* fashion. He also points out, following Chief Rabbi Goren, that the key element of Sanhedrin is its representative authority.[10] Furthermore, the *urim ve-tumim* is no longer necessary for consultation now that it is defunct, according to some authorities.[11]

The Sanhedrin would provide a counter-balance to the ruler(s) in making the decision to go to war, thus balancing state interest and the people's interests (though not those of the adversaries) in deciding to go to war.[12] In the immediate background of this formulation, especially regarding Kimelman's citation of Chief Rabbi Goren, seems to be a suggested justification of war making in contemporary Israel when the elected government and recognized *halakhic* leaders agree on going to war, though I am uncertain of this. There appears, however, to be some confidence that the agreement of the state and the representative *halakhic* body would be enough to ensure that the war is conducted for "moral" reasons.

It must be noted, however, that Kimelman, like many previous scholars, weds this argument to an extensive effort to circumscribe both the legitimization of war and the conduct of war by a broad series of ethical/*halakhic* guidelines. This includes not engaging in wars that will involve more than one-sixth of one's forces as casualties, allowing escape routes for retreating forces, and conducting negotiations before besieging a city,

---

10 Kimelman, *War, supra* note 6, at 312.

11 *Id.* at n.16.

12 *Id.* at 312–313.

"calling out to it in peace first." Destruction that is unnecessary for the achievement of military aims is disallowed. Destruction of the surrounding environment is not allowed. The killing of noncombatants is not allowed.[13]

This raises an issue, not really addressed by Kimelman, namely, the problematic nature of targeting anything near civilian populations with explosive weapons. In general, I would argue, explosive weapons, from rocket launched grenades to F-16's, and certainly weapons of mass destruction, make it extremely difficult to comply, in any contemporary warfare, with the *halakhic* rule that requires giving even combatants, let alone unarmed civilians, a way out of conflict, a path of retreat.

It would seem that Kimelman hopes to limit war due to the nature of the *halakhic* institutions that would need to support a war, and which in some fashion represent the interests of the people. In principle I would agree that getting the consent to go to war from those who represent the average person's interests is no longer easy in an age where the brutality of war is available in the living room of every parent who would send a child to the battlefield. But a present-day *halakhic* body would not necessarily be the equivalent of a democratic or even representative institution by any means, especially in a largely nonreligious and at times anti-religious society in Israel. On the other hand, the Israeli Parliament, which *is* a representative elected body hardly operates in terms of *halakhic* guidelines on issues of national security and morality surrounding the taking of life, nor can its members in any way be seen as having *halakhic* authority. Thus, we are still left without a clear way to conduct a modern Jewish war, or even a mechanism to determine which wars are justified.

David Novak, reflecting on a Jewish attitude to wars conducted by gentiles, which Jews must decide whether to support (specifically regarding the Vietnam war), employs the *rodef* law, made infamous by the assas-

---

[13] These guidelines raise several issues. First, one-sixth of one's mobilized forces in modern warfare involves a huge amount of deaths. For example, there were 8,744,000 American forces mobilized in Vietnam. One-sixth dead would have meant approximately 1.5 million American deaths. Fifty-eight thousand actual American casualties caused a significant crisis in the social history of the United States. Great Britain, in one of its most devastating social traumas in its history, lost approximately one-eighth of its armed forces, one million men out of eight million mobilized in W.W. I. *See* The 1994 INFORMATION PLEASE ALMANAC, 385, 389 (1994). Furthermore, there is no mention in the Jewish sources of a limit on enemy soldier deaths. Thus there would be no moral calculation regarding 2 million Vietnamese dead versus 58,000 American dead, or 180,000 Iraqi deaths due to the war and the embargo (this is a rough approximation that includes mostly noncombatants who died due to the destruction of the electric infrastructure, hospital supplies etc. These numbers are still debated.) versus about 100 American deaths. However, there would be a serious *halakhic* problem with the number of those dead who were non-combatants, the massive use of napalm, an indiscriminate weapon, and the lack of escape routes from carpet bombing campaigns.

sination of the late Prime Minister Rabin. The *rodef* law requires a person A to intervene and stop B from killing C. But A may not use any means whatever, unless it is clear that killing B is the only way to stop him. And, in fact, A can be guilty of murder if he does not need to use deadly force. This law is used rabbinically to justify abortion where the fetus is threatening the life of the mother. The assassin of Rabin and his rabbis[14] extended this law to politics, and made the case that, in their mind, Rabin was a direct and immediate threat to Jewish life, a position that the vast majority of rabbinic authorities have repudiated.

Novak extends this law to justify exactly the opposite of killing regarding Vietnam. If persons B and C, argues Novak, are not clearly defined, and we do not know who exactly is trying to kill whom, then the law of *rodef* does not apply, and another *halakhic* principle, namely, not destroying one life for another, or not considering one life more valuable than another, becomes morally paramount. Who was really the pursuer in this Vietnamese war is dubious from an ethical point of view, argues Novak. Whether it was a war of aggression by the North, a civil war, or the Cold War fought by proxy, or all three, is unclear. Furthermore, the United States was hardly in a position to make a moral judgment on this, considering the fact that its strategic interests were paramount, and its decisions about the war were certainly not based on the Jewish law of *rodef*.[15] Thus it would be very complicated to justify the war as a religious Jew, argues Novak.

I would point out the rather circumscribed nature of the *rodef* law in that it only justifies use of force in very limited circumstances of "hot pursuit," as far as I have been able to tell.[16] The danger of the political extension of this law to war and wholesale killing, or the use of this law to justify pre-meditated killing when there is no hot pursuit seems clear. Thus while Novak's use of the *rodef* law to limit the justification of war is understandable, I think that its extension at all by theorists to situations beyond "hot pursuit" of one person by another that you see before you is ill-advised.[17] It confuses political calculus and the *halakhic* chal-

---

14 Who these rabbis were or whether anyone specifically authorized Amir is a matter of debate, because everyone denies *ex post facto* that they supported assassination, despite their rhetoric beforehand.

15 David Novak, Law and Theology in Judaism 130 (1974).

16 The context in the following sources seems clearly limited to "hot pursuit" circumstances: T.B. Bava Kama 117b; T.B. Sanhedrin 72b; Maimonides, *Mishneh Torah*, Hilkhot Nizke Mammon 9:6; *id.*, Hilkhot Rotseah 1:6–7.

17 The abortion analogy would still be valid based on my analysis of *rodef*. The rabbis suggested that a caretaker, seeing that the fetus before them is threatening the mother, must then see the fetus as a *rodef*, and protect the mother at the expense of the fetus. This does not extend the killing justification beyond the immediate circumstances, however.

lenges of individual decisionmaking in very particular situations.

There seems to be very little to justify Jewish war today, except when being attacked, and even then a set of circumscribing *jus in bello* laws apply. It is also not clear to me whether even this category is legitimate, because the state of Israel is not a *halakhically* constituted state. Neither were the many Jewish communities in the pre-modern era. The very category of *halakhic* war is only discussed by the Mishnaic and Talmudic rabbis in the context of a highly theoretical construct of the *halakhic* state. Many rabbinic discussions in general—most of the discussions in certain areas of law, in fact—are completely theoretical in nature because the current circumstances make the law's applicability impossible. I am not satisfied that it has been proven that these Talmudic war discussions apply to any circumstances beyond the Second Temple period, or could in principle. Furthermore, it is questionable whether the rabbis, even in the period of the second Temple, ever had a sovereign construct in which their guidelines to war were ever operationalized.

This leaves us with two curiously overlooked Jewish principles. One is that saving of life, *pikuah nefesh*,[18] justifies the abrogation of most other laws, and the other is the principle that if someone comes to kill you, you are obligated to kill him first in self-defense.[19] As far as the former, one is permitted to do almost anything to save one's life and the lives of others, with the exception of incest, idolatry, and pre-meditated murder. However, I cannot kill someone else who is not attacking me. Thus, even if person A, ordering me to kill person B, will kill me instead if I do not comply, I cannot follow the order. Now it is clear that war is a very different situation from this, where an attacking army is directly threatening one's life, and the lives of many others. The people that I kill are the people who are attacking. Once again, however, it would be very problematic to kill civilians or those not directly threatening one's life, based on this law, say with indiscriminate bombardment of enemy cities. The same would apply to the second rule. These two principles seem to me to justify the use of violence in very *limited* circumstances of attack, and makes organized war that operates in an environment of many civilians very problematic.

INDIVIDUAL RELIGIOUS ETHICS VERSUS RELIGIOUS WARFARE

This limited notion of self-defense in specific circumstances highlights the way in which Jewish law and religion is supremely wedded to individual circumstance. This has ramifications in terms of the following. One of the fundamental challenges to the moral evaluation of war in general, not just Jewish war, is the way in which the word "war" includes

---

18 *See, for example, Shulhan Arukh*, Orah Hayyim 160:22; 248:41; 329:1.

19 *See, for example,* T.B. Berakhot 58a; T.B. Sanhedrin 72a.

such a vast array of unpredictable circumstances, especially modern war. How is the individual who is committed to a personal code of morality expected to suspend all of those values in the context of war? When is the personal code, or one's *halakhic* code in the Jewish situation, to be suspended and when is it not to be suspended? When does the obligation to kill, steal or destroy things as a part of warfare, override all of the everyday laws that absolutely prohibit these activities? When exactly is there a suspension of the numerous *halakhic* moral safeguards governing one's internal life and external behavior that often prohibit even the hint of violence, such as talebearing or losing one's temper?

Michael Walzer attempts to get at some of these issues by looking at the details of war situations, but it is a very difficult enterprise.[20] The same is true of the dichotomy between extremely high standards of conduct demanded by Halakha and Jewish pietistic literature as applied to individuals versus the behavior that is apparently acceptable and expected in war. We see from Kimelman's sources that indeed the rabbis expected some complex interaction between these two spheres. But the interaction remains extremely nebulous, as far as I can tell, as if there is a vacuum of experience in this regard. Indeed, rabbinic Judaism has had little experience of organized warfare in the last two thousand years where Jews are the combatants, not the victims. The vast chasm between the life of warfare and the Talmudic and medieval pietistic insistence on an utterly sanctified day to day, even moment to moment, interpersonal lifestyle seems to be insufficiently confronted.

Let us take an example. Person A is part of a group that has expressed hostility to *some* Jews at some point in time, such as Christians in medieval Europe, or Arabs today, but has not attacked a Jew himself. Does one treat person A as an enemy, as if war has been declared, or does one, on the contrary, owe him all of the moral obligations of the Jewish tradition: honoring him as a creature of God, or as an elder (if he is older), greeting him with peace, honoring his property, even loving him as a creature of God, as Hillel did to all gentiles,[21] and so on? Is this stranger perhaps in an in-between state? How can one immediately classify all Christians, Arabs, or Muslims in one category, simply because some of them at some point in time have engaged in hostilities? How does one determine the contours of enemy, friend, righteous gentile, and, most importantly from a realistic as well as psychological point of view, those who are in-between, neither friend nor foe. These questions are particularly relevant today to Jewish-Arab relations, for example, but have never really been analyzed in Jewish legal tradition, due to reasons that wait to be uncovered.

---

20 Michael Walzer, Just and Unjust Wars (1977). *See especially* Parts 4 and 5.

21 *See* Mishnah Avot 1:12; The Fathers According to Rabbi Nathan Ch. 12.

A far deeper problem with the secondary literature on war in Judaism is that it suffers from a compartmentalized and fragmented approach to life. It is only one part of a religious system of belief and practice that actually governs all human interactions. But the literature reads as if the question of war and violence can be discussed and then acted upon utterly divorced from the rest of Jewish morality. In this way, it models itself on discussions of *jus ad bellum* and *jus in bello* in Christian tradition that have a long history. The latter, however, may be accused of the same thing. Both discussions divorce the subject of war from the rest of the range of religious values applied to the individual, as if these other religious values, such as humility, compassion, and justice, which are incumbent on the individual, were abolished during war or irrelevant to the decision of whether to participate in a war, or whether there are other avenues of dealing with adversaries short of war, and as if the Jewish moral agent somehow disappears on the battlefield. Most importantly for our subject, regarding the transition from war to peace or peace to war, it is as if the decision to engage in war with an enemy is somehow divorced from the entire set of human interactions that brings groups of people to the brink of conflict, violence and bloodshed.

Here is the most important point. War does not happen in a vacuum without any causal chain leading to it. Furthermore, war is not neatly separated from other human interactions. War is first a distant possibility, then it becomes one, and then it disappears again. Or it grows, is waged, but suddenly stops due to any number of complex socio-economic, psychodynamic, and political factors. In other words, whether war happens, how it proceeds, and how and why it ends is a sufficiently complex human phenomenon that it cannot be separated from the range of human choices and behaviors that lead up to it, or interact with it in complex ways. There are innumerable contributing factors that bring people to a state of war, and these factors themselves, be they political, economic, psychological or ethical, can be further broken down to many individual choices that helped create the atmosphere of war. These innumerable individual choices are precisely the kind of choices that most interest rabbinic *halakhic* Judaism, especially the sources that ask continually, "What brings people to bloodshed?" But this aspect of *halakhic* thinking does not become part of the *halakhic* analysis of war in the scholarly literature.

It is also clear from our experience in conflict analysis and intervention that war often exists along a continuum from deeply embedded friendship, to miscommunication, to peaceful but cool co-existence, to serious disagreement, small-scale isolated conflict, large-scale isolated conflict turning into chronic conflict, isolated bloodshed, organized massive bloodshed, and sometimes genocide. This continuum is in itself complex, and it does not always follow a predictable order. But this more nuanced understanding of warmaking as well as peacemaking means that many of the circumstances leading up to war are, in fact, governed morally by other parts of Jewish moral and *halakhic* tradition that apply directly to the individual and to the spiritual community (the *kehillah* in the medieval and modern period), not just a sovereign or a Sanhedrin. The latter emerge as more important when being attacked. But even afterward they do not supplant the individual's moral decisionmaking in key choices that he makes on the battlefield, as we have seen.

Far too little attention is given, by contrast, to all of the circumstances leading up to attacking or being attacked, how to avoid a conflict that turns into war, what religious values prevent conflict and bloodshed, or what to do when the war or acts of violence are over in terms of mourning, recovery and reconciliation, and the moral laws and values that come into play for this crucial stage of human relations. Yet rabbinic sources are filled with advice on these matters, but this is somehow cut off in the secondary literature from the war discussion. This is a distortion—though probably not conscious—of the complex panorama of rabbinic Judaism.

It cannot be denied that just war efforts from the pre-modern era to limit war are laudable. We now know from recent experience with the 20th century penchant for terror through the targeting of civilians that agreed upon *jus in bello* limits would be a major advance on many war situations around the world. If enemies agreed, for example, to limit war to men in uniform, to eliminate rape as a weapon, to eliminate children from being subjects or objects of warfare, to agree to eliminate sacred sites and city centers from bombing targets, we would eliminate the vast majority of the barbarism into which the world descended in the 20th century. The more experience I have in conflict intervention the more I have come to welcome the value of these pre-modern standards as the basis for step-by-step bilateral confidence-building measures between bitter enemies.

I often ask myself why there were pre-modern wars in which these limits were adhered to, but which all fell apart in the 20th century. Sometimes I suspect that it is the very pacifist illusions of the post-World War I era that led to a kind of psychological and ethical unpreparedness for the barbaric potential of war that increased exponentially due to technology. Air war, light weapons, unconventional weapons, and remote control all made barbarism and terrorism very easy, practically the flick of a switch. The human species was unprepared for this power. At the same time we developed delusions of a world without war and were thus unprepared to limit our own brutality.

That having been said, and now that we are in this place of very complex, very deadly conflict, we must maximize our creative use of the individual, and his or her moral capacity to anticipate, prevent and heal conflicts. If there is a silver lining to the last several hundred years of technological advance that have made it so easy to be barbaric, it is the fact that a slow and steady march of democratization has infected this planet.

Due to technology of communication, millions of people are empowered more than ever before to engage in cross-cultural, cross-religious, and international relationship building. Elitist diplomacy, shackled by a desperate fear of the dissolution of the state as such, has viewed the individual's foray into the area of conflict prevention and resolution with trepidation and suspicion. This has resulted in a fantastic waste of cultural and spiritual resources for the construction of global civilization.

It is quite clear that the subtleties of individual religious ethical values and relationship building processes can and should play a much larger role in future processes of conflict resolution. This may very well provide nations or groups with the ability to prevent conflicts from becoming wars, and, alternatively, help wars to become constructive conflicts.[22] These values are paramount: respect for all human beings as God's creatures, the ethics of interpersonal encounter and respect, training in the capacity to admit mistakes, regret the past, apologize, repent, and promise a different future, compassion wedded to and in struggle with strict justice, a commitment to pursuit of peace as a religious experience, humility, the skills of respectful listening and silence.[23]

We need to look forward to a future in which we recognize the potential of religious individuals and communities to play a pivotal role in conflict prevention and resolution. We dare not create our own nightmare by assuming and insisting that ultra-violent constructs of religious traditions are its authentic core, while peacemaking constructs are apologetic appendages. The lived religion of millions of human beings, past and present, suggest that religious human beings can play a pivotal role in not only the advocacy of peace, but also the subtle insertion of peace into the inner recesses of damaged human relationships. This is a level of peacemaking and healing before which just war theory and interna-

---

22 "Constructive conflict" refers to those conflicts that lead by their nature to a better state of human affairs. Human beings must engage in conflicts to defend their interests or those of others, in other words, to defend justice. But how they do this, and what the response is, decides whether the dynamics of the conflict are constructive or destructive. Humanitarian intervention causes conflict with those who may not want the aid to take place, or who may want to take the aid for themselves. Nevertheless, the aid must be given. On the other hand, humanitarian intervention should be always accompanied by the best methods of conflict resolution in order to minimize the loss of human life, which is the ultimate goal.

23 For a full paradigm of the ethics of conflict resolution out of the sources of religion, *see* MARC GOPIN, BETWEEN EDEN AND ARMAGEDDON: THE FUTURE OF WORLD RELIGIONS, VIOLENCE AND PEACEMAKING Chs. 2 and 7 (2000). For a paradigm out of the sources of Jewish communal and individual ethics, *see id.*, Chs. 5 and 8. On constructs of conflict resolution in the Abrahamic traditions as they pertain to the Palestinian/Israeli conflict, *see* HOLY WAR, HOLY PEACE: HOW RELIGION CAN BRING PEACE TO THE MIDDLE EAST (2000).

tional relations theory should deferentially bow. It may be the only antidote we can evolve as a species that will counteract the indescribable power that technology has placed in the service of human anger. Whether it be small bombs on the backs of 19-year-old suicides, light weapons in the hands of teenagers from Liberia to American high schools, we need much deeper skills of conflict resolution and healing than ever before in human history. The time is not near that we as civilization seem capable of banning these weapons, as obvious a solution as this is. As an alternative, religious cultures and their ethical traditions need to be given a chance to respond to violence and war in creative conjunction with other forms of diplomacy and social science intervention.

CONCLUSIONS

Let us draw some conclusions. The war laws of self-defense in Judaism may or may not apply to many of the complex circumstances of modern political and military choices. It certainly is possible to declare that a defensive war is a positive commandment in certain circumstances, but these circumstances are not very likely today. It certainly does not offer particularly helpful guides in terms of humanitarian intervention and the use of force.

What is clear is that the saving of human lives is a critical and overarching principle that can be useful for our investigation. The saving of human lives (*pikuah nefesh*) is an ultimate value in Jewish tradition. What maximizes the saving of human lives in complex situations of hostility, or potential hostility? What saves the most lives when weighing in the balance humanitarian intervention, conflict resolution and the use of force? These are the essential questions we face pragmatically but also in terms of our religious ethical dilemmas.

The best of conflict resolution practices are designed to minimize the loss of life. They also are designed to maximize the combination of peace and justice. If they are applied early and well they will eliminate the need for most wars. Nevertheless, it must be admitted that (1) there are groups of human beings determined to kill mercilessly, and (2) we face choices in the world where, whether we like it or not, the best practices of conflict prevention were never applied early enough to a violent situation. And now we are faced with choices involving the use of force as part of humanitarian intervention.

It seems to me that every step of the process leading to the use of force must involve careful calculations as to whether its benefits will save more innocent lives than it costs. And the costs and ripple effects of violence and war are well known. This seems to me to be the best way to engage the lessons of Jewish ethics for conflict prevention, management, and humanitarian intervention. *Pikuah nefesh* should be the primary barometer by which to evaluate alternative courses of action. It may be the case that sometimes the use of force will save lives, while in most circumstances it seems to create a cycle that loses more lives than it saves. Nevertheless, protection of the innocent is the key.

Most deep analysis of conflict comes to the conclusion that most wars could have been prevented if attention was paid early on to their deeper causes. Thus, with *pikuah nefesh* as its focus, Jewish legal tradition should demand early and sustained conflict prevention as part and parcel of diplomacy and humanitarian intervention. Nevertheless, if one reaches a place and time in which lives are being lost by the failure to use effective force, then *pikuah nefesh* demands aggressive action. Both by the standards of Jewish just war tradition, as well as the moral calculus of *pikuah nefesh*, such aggressive action should cause a minimum of damage to bystanders. Furthermore, it should be accompanied by an equally aggressive conflict resolution campaign that reaches out to enemy populations with aid and gestures of peace, all in order to consistently separate hardened criminals and perpetrators of violence from their indigenous communities.

There is a vital role for people-to-people diplomacy in this work. The principal locus of Jewish ethics is in interpersonal relations and values. Therefore, humanitarian intervention in a subtle combination with conflict management must be informed by a range of Jewish religious values, including humility, compassion, and honor and respect. The dilemmas must be faced with attention to a balance of key commandments, such as the pursuit of peace, the pursuit of justice, as well as the aforementioned *pikuah nefesh*.

The popular, people-to-people work, however, must be accompanied by an attention to the power and importance of religious leadership. Religious leaders have a special responsibility to provide a paradigm of careful religious decisionmaking. For example, the words that they use, and the way that they frame their teachings can have a dramatic impact on how force is used or not used by devoutly religious soldiers or police. Often they have an even broader cultural impact on those who are not religious but who, when facing ethical dilemmas involving force and conflict, may turn to religious leaders for inspiration. Religious leaders can also play a key role in diplomacy, especially when secular political leaders are stuck in an impasse.

In conclusion, it seems clear that Jewish law and tradition about war as such may not be directly relevant to present day circumstances. But a host of other moral values that are part of Judaism are directly relevant to facing the ethical dilemmas surrounding humanitarian intervention, the use of force, and the resolution of violent conflicts.

CHAPTER 2

FROM DEFENSIVE TO OFFENSIVE WARFARE: THE USE AND ABUSE OF *JIHAD* IN THE MUSLIM WORLD

*Dr. Abdulaziz A. Sachedina**

INTRODUCTION

In the wake of September 11, 2001, the issues in this chapter take on a new meaning. But the basic issues remain the same: what is the nature of Islamic thinking about international military action, and how may an understanding of that thinking help us to appreciate why both states and sub-state groups intervene in other states and to what end. Obviously, the central focus of this inquiry must be on the idea of *jihad* and the course that thinking about that idea has taken over the whole history of Islam. We should, however, begin at the end by noting that post-colonial conditions in the Muslim world have fostered interpretations of *jihad* which lead to meaningless violence rather than to the Islamic goal of building a just society. Unfortunately, we cannot argue that these interpretations are invalid, only that they were formulated in an earlier time, to deal with a very different set of circumstances. Their appropriation today by extremist Muslims enables these individuals to call for *jihad* in tones, and often in terms, that provide rationales for greater violence against enemies than the classic juristic discourse would seem to sanction.

This is, in my opinion, a consequence of history. The Muslim legal-theological discourses were articulated in order to highlight the Qur'anic message about "*islam* (submission) being the only true religion with God" (K 3:19) and the only one desired by God (K 3:85) to which end it would have a dominant political and social position in the community. Initially, as I shall show later, such armed actions as Muslims took were for their defense (or that of co-religionists in adjacent areas) against persecution—though the measures employed included offensive operations such as raids, skirmishes and sieges of others cities, as well as the defense of Medina.

* Department of Religious Studies, University of Virginia.

However, the interaction between the exclusivist idea of Islam as the one true and sufficient religion for all humanity, and the existing predominance of the Muslim empire in the era when the idea of *jihad* gained its definitive shape, created the specific juridical-theological language that provides the normative justification to extend the notion of *jihad* beyond its strictly defensive meaning in the Qur'an to its being justification for offensive actions aimed at the hegemonic expansion of the Muslim empire. Thus, while we may appropriate the language of *jihad*, and the tradition of thought behind it, to develop a distinctly Muslim approach to and endorsement of humanitarian intervention, such an appropriation is fraught with dangers to which we must remain alert—not the least of them being that Muslims may be the only appropriate beneficiaries of such intervention.

First, some definitional matters. I refer throughout this chapter to discourses on *jihad* in three different eras of the history of Islamic thought. First of all I speak of the period of early Islam, as captured in the Qur'an, which speaks in response to pre-Islamic tribal culture. Secondly, I speak of the period of the Caliphate, during which time the debates about *jihad* expanded, and altered, the meaning of that term quite significantly. Finally, I speak of contemporary Islam, in which we are faced with the difficulty of determining how to go forward in using the concept of *jihad* given its complex history.

Similarly, in this chapter I use the word "Islam" in three senses. In the Western studies of Islam, the term "Islam" is primarily used in the meaning of a religious tradition whose fundamental normative principles (or creed) provide authoritative perspectives for interpreting contradictions and tensions in human existence. I have retained this usage whenever I deal with normative sources for the derivation of justifications as well as criteria for *jihad*. But I also use the term "Islam" to signify an important ingredient in the formation of those cultural values that permeate the dispositions and practices connected with *jihad* as practiced in a specific time and place. Finally, I use the term to convey an overarching ideological system that, in the name of a sacred authority, provides justifications for the creation of a particular type of state as a means to promoting the common good. In a way, the three senses—covering the beliefs, attitudes, and practices of the community—demonstrate the intricate developing relationship, within the context of sociopolitical history, between the authoritative and determinative teachings of Islam and the emerging power of the state that undertakes to implement these teachings for the creation of an ideal public order.

The ultimate outcome of this historical interplay between Islam as a religion and Islam as a source of power is also reflected in the way the community has sought to overcome the obstacles to the realization of the idealized vision of a religious polity on earth. In other words, the idea of *jihad* (in its essential meaning of "struggle" and "striving") as an instrument for realizing the Islamic ideal on earth has had to interact with the sociopolitical realities that confronted the Muslims when responding to its call for struggle in the name of a sacred authority. Like Judaism and Christianity, Islam recognized the ordinary moral needs and abilities of the common people, while still insisting that all should work for an ideal, just society. This outlook stressed the active involvement of the people in creating a public order that would reflect the moral and social teachings of Islam. In this sense, Islam (in its primary meaning of being a religious tradition) inherently functioned as an "activist" ideology, existing critically within a specific social-political system, calling upon its followers to defend and preserve or to overthrow and transform it. However, as the third sense should make clear, Islam was understood as a divine blueprint that demands implementation to realize God's will on earth to the fullest extent possible and, if necessary, through force—that is, through armed *jihad*.

THE HISTORY OF *JIHAD* BEFORE MODERNITY

Insofar as the Qur'an, the foundational source for Muslim social-political consciousness, introduced the legitimate use of force through the idea of *jihad*, it was responding to the pre-Islamic Arab tribal culture, which had institutionalized military power as the element on which depended the security of a tribe and even its existence. Primacy among the tribes belonged to those that were able to protect all their clients and to avenge all insults, injuries, and deaths through their military strength. The Semitic system of retaliatory justice based on "a life for a life" could not always ensure that crime could—or would—be punished. Against this background, the legitimate use of force commanded by the Qur'an was merely to provide appropriate moral restrictions on the use of military power to promote tribal influence and advance tribal interests. Legitimation of *jihad*, in the sense of "fighting," appears in the context of defending the community and halting the breakdown of the public order so that "there is no persecution and the religion be only for God" (K. 2:193). This was a prescriptive measure to arrest the harm caused to the community at large and to redress the wrongs suffered by the weak at the hands of those who sought to thwart the divine purpose on earth. The use of force, as far as the Qur'an is concerned, is defensive and limited to correcting the violation of those rights authorized and directed by Allah. It is crucial to emphasize the Qur'an's defensive strategy in dealing with the problem of violence stemming from human rejection of Islam.

My categorization of the Qur'anic *jihad* as strictly defensive is based on the absolute absence of any reference to an offensive *jihad* in the Qur'an, that is, *jihad* undertaken to convert all humanity to Islam. But the Qur'an does not stop at this duty of self-defense against hostile forces. It leaves open the possibility of offensive *jihad* when it requires the Prophet to strive to create an ideal public order. And as the historical development of the relationship between Islam and power progressed, post-Qur'anic Muslim jurists regarded this explicitly Qur'anic principle of defensive warfare as abrogated by the so-called "sword verse" (Q. 9:5) that declares war on the unbelievers: ". . . slay them wherever you find them, and take them, and confine them, and lie in wait for them at every place of ambush." They maintained that fighting was obligatory for Muslims, even when the unbelievers had not begun hostilities.

At this point, the *jihad* became an offensive struggle to bring about the kind of world order envisioned by Islam. The legitimation of an offensive *jihad* as a device for the creation of the Islamic world order gives rise to the tension between the tolerance advocated in matters relating to the religious destiny of human beings, and the active response required against those disbelievers who persecute Muslims.[1] The development of Muslim political power provides a warrant for wars of expansion, depending upon how one interprets the passages of the Qur'an that speak about fighting the hostile unbelievers "until there is no persecution and the religion be only for God" (K. 2:191). This accommodation with the historical practice of *jihad* is not uncommon in the works of the jurists. In the wake of the phenomenal conquests achieved by Muslim armies during the seventh century, the jurists began to apply the term *jihad* to military action and to efforts to extend the boundaries of the Islamic polity[2] through expanding the Muslim Empire.

The classical understanding of *jihad* was secured when Muslims were in power and when emphasis on the exclusivist doctrine contrived from the Qur'anic verse was seen more in political terms: "We have sent you [o Muhammad] not, except to humankind entire (*kaffatu'n-nas*), good tidings to bear, and warning" (Q. 34:27). The Muslim juristic-theological discourses that legitimated a militarized and offensive *jihad* were created to justify the claims of conquering Muslim armies that "Islam is the only true religion with God" (Q. 3:19) and the only one desired by God (Q. 3:85). These provided the divinely ordained mandate for the offensive *jihad* with the goal being Islam's successful political and social domination of the whole human community. This interaction—between the idea of Islam being the universal religion for all humankind and the empirically apparent predominance of Muslim political power, especially in its early centuries—created the specific legal language that provided the justification

1 I have discussed the Qur'anic pluralism in my recently published study, THE ISLAMIC ROOTS OF DEMOCRATIC PLURALISM (2001).

2 See: Khaled Abu El Fadl, "*Akham al-Bughat:* Irregular Warfare and the Law of Rebellion in Islam," in *Cross, Crescent and Sword: The Justification and Limitation of War in Western and Islamic Tradition*, ed. James T. Johnson and John Kelsay (New York: Greenwood Press, 1990), pp. 129–176.

to extend the notion of *jihad* beyond its strictly defensive meaning in the Qur'an to its being an offensive instrument for the Muslim creation of a dominant political order.

Under the classical juristic discourse the limitations set upon the conduct of warfare against Muslims and non-Muslims were not the same. If Muslims fight other Muslims, there are binding regulations that do not necessarily apply to Muslims fighting non-Muslims. If Muslims fight one another, the fugitive and wounded may not be dispatched. Muslim prisoners may not be executed or enslaved. Children and women may not be intentionally killed or imprisoned. Imprisoned male Muslims must be released once the fighting, or the danger of continued fighting, ends. Even more, strategies of mass destruction may not be used unless absolutely necessary.

In principle, Muslims are prohibited from fighting each other; if they do, they are considered to have committed a grave sin. Muslim jurists in general cautioned against the evil of rash and violent rebellions even against unjust rulers.[3] (It is important to emphasize that Muslim jurists base the treatment of Muslim combatants on the perceived moral culpability of those who were the cause of social unrest, but most of their efforts focused on the morality of conduct and not the morality of purpose.) As for issues related to the fighting against non-Muslims, its legality was not discussed because the doctrine of the finality of the Islamic revelation and its universality for all humankind was taken as a given. Muslim jurists conceded to the ruler the authority to negotiate relations with foreign powers, keeping in mind the protection of Muslims under their domain. However, the rules about the conduct of war were not very different from those that applied to the Muslim rebels engaged in fighting an unjust Muslim ruler. All proper limits that applied to the "in family" Muslims fighting Muslims were articulated for conducting war against non-Muslims to whom the jurists also imputed a degree of moral culpability.

In sum, in the classical period, Muslim juristic discourse regarding *jihad* became a thoroughly legitimating discourse, justifying the undertaking of the *jihad* as a divinely ordained duty, with a prescription to expand the sphere of Muslim dominions, assuring Muslim warriors of their reward in this and the next world for fulfilling the duty of fighting in the path of God. Although one can observe the attempt to strike a balance between conservative legitimation and aspiration generated by simple fidelity to the inherited doctrines and precedents of a juristic culture, more often than not this discourse tended to be based on an imperfect understanding of a changed textual reality that required a practical or functional response—either one that tried to assess what is actually feasible,

---

3 *See* KHALID ABU EL FADL, *supra* note 2, at 161–63.

or one that took into account the potential requirement of maintaining an Islamic order.[4]

From this brief history, several general claims may be made. First of all, it is certainly the case that, while there may be significant differences and even tensions between the general viewpoints, something like a "just-war tradition" exists within Islamic thought. A number of Muslim scholars have questioned the pre-modern juridical formulations about *jihad* and declared them incompatible with the international norms that govern the laws of war.[5] But at the same time other Muslim scholars have argued that the antecedents for the just war tradition's concerns with proportionality and discrimination in war—which in turn contributed to the rise of humanitarian law—are embedded in Islamic conceptions of *jihad*. After all, the normative idea of communal *jihad* was very much a rule-governed activity: *jihad* was conceived as a collective obligation of the *dar al-islam* against the *dar al-harb*, under the authority and direction of the designated successor of the Prophet Mohammad (a concept which was held by jurists of both the Sunni and Shii persuasions early on, though they differed as to who was the proper successor to the Prophet and thus head of the Muslim community). The focus of pre-modern juridical discussion of *jihad* was on elaborating criteria of *jus in bello*—concerns with the principles of discrimination (or noncombatant immunity) and proportionality in use of force in warfare. However, while the legality of engaging in warfare was ultimately taken as established through the historical precedents which showed *jihad* to be both a war of defense as well as a war for territorial expansion, there were serious *jus ad bellum* requirements as well: right authority (the successor to the Prophet), just cause (the threat posed by the *dar al-harb*), right intention (pursuit of the Qur'anic ideal of promoting good and forbidding evil by actively aiming to spread the rule of Islamic law), reasonable hope of success (the Caliph/Imam is to chose carefully when and where to initiate jihad, so

---

[4] For instance, a Muslim jurist may write that a permanent state of peace may not exist between Muslims and non-Muslims, and that non-Muslims should be fought at least once a year. The jurists might believe that their statement accurately describes an actual practice of their community, or that it responds to a practical concern. If the ruling is based on a reading of a context suggesting a political and social reality, then it is a functional ruling to accomplish a specific result. If non-Muslims are not aggressively fighting Muslims, or if attacking non-Muslims once a year will not produce the desired effect of inspiring fear in non-Muslims, then the rule is simply in the books waiting to be implemented. Yet the jurist's imperfect understanding of his own reality, or a change in circumstances, might reveal that, more than anything else, this statement was meant to be prescriptive in nature, that is, it lays down what is desirable in every setting. In this case, the statement is a moral prescription, the rule remains valid, regardless of the consequences or results, and non-Muslims, as desired by the lawgiver, should be attacked at least once a year.

[5] Muhammad Sa'id al-Ashmawi, al-Islam al-Siyasi (1987).

that success is likely), the end of peace (spread of the rule of [Islamic] law), and so on.

But the differences between Islamic and "Western" (really, Christian and post-Christian) positions on just war do need to be explicitly confronted and addressed. Most importantly for the purposes of this book, Islam sees no (or very little) basis for waging war except the expansion of the realm of peace (*dar-al-Islam*). This combines moral and religious motivations in powerful, but potentially problematic ways. Because of the moral connection through the idea of "peace," the criteria may be developed in fruitful ways; nevertheless, any such development must be careful and complex, because of the religious implications packed into the idea of "peace" in Islam. (It is an open question whether these implications could be "sorted out" or rather simply distinguished, and left commingled.)

We will see, however, that the sorts of "development" undertaken by many contemporary radical Muslim thinkers are precisely the sort of development that we do *not* need. So I turn to that next.

JIHAD IN THE MODERN AGE

Almost a thousand years have passed since the Caliphate flourished, years which have witnessed enormous changes in the position and importance of Islam. Even as the doctrine gained new concepts and spread to lands of which Mohammad had probably never heard, the political unity of Islam was shattered, by differences among Muslim rulers, by invasions of the Turkic tribes and by the Mongol invasions; even the far-flung Ottoman Empire could not bring together all those peoples who believed in the Prophet. And in more recent years, these early enemies have been replaced by the even more powerful nations of Europe, powerful not just because of their political organization, their technology and their military effectiveness, but because of their economies and their cultures. Indeed, it is the latter, even more than the former, that threaten the Muslim way of life today—and have called forth, among other responses, a new definition of *jihad.*

Thus, the *fatwas* issued in modern times reminding Muslims about their religious duty to undertake *jihad* show an important shift from classical rulings about engagement in war against non-Muslims. One change is that whereas the classical juristic discourse reflected how Muslim jurists aspired to provide justifications for engaging in *jihad* with non-Muslims as part of the divinely ordained activity to bring all of humanity under Islamic dominion, the modern *fatwas* call for radical resistance to the Western "aggression" against Muslim peoples.[6] In some sense this is a

---

[6] In recent history the call for *jihad* has been heard coming from both religious as well as secular Muslim leaders, fighting sometimes external aggression or domination, and

reflection of the shift in the balance of power over the past thousand years. In some sense it is an acknowledgement of the pressures of "globalization" upon a lifestyle which is still patriarchal and in some respects "out of sync" with that in countries that are not dominated by fundamentalist Muslims. Thus, Muslims today, like those of ancient Medina, are again on the defensive.

Another change is that the conduct of *jihad* is seen as a responsibility of individual Muslims and not of a polity that no longer exists, directed by a Caliph who no longer sits upon the throne.[7] This approach derives from an earlier juristic conception, in which the authority to resist aggression in an emergency lies not with the Caliph/Imam but with every individual Muslim who is in a position to do so. What has happened is that this *emergency* concept of *jihad* has become the *normative* concept. And this means of course, that there can be many different justifications for *jihad.*

Furthermore, modern statements on *jihad* not only provide justifications for going to war different from the classical ones but also advocate terrorism and individual acts of violence against the enemy, civilian or otherwise, wherever they may be found in the world. Thus, Usama bin Laden, in his *fatwa* of 1998, justified terrorist acts against the United States as a response to aggressive American policy towards Muslims in general, and its support of the corrupt Saudi regime. He regards *jihad* as an individual duty (*fard'ayn*), which must be performed by all male, able-bodied Muslims, and not simply a collective one (*fard kifaya*), which, if performed by a sufficient number, relieves others from the obligation of performing it. Bin Laden goes even further to argue that terrorism is a legitimate and morally demanded duty so long as anti-Muslim forces are carrying arms in Muslim lands, especially Muslim holy places. This argument for terrorism as a legitimate means of conduct in war is a clear departure from the classical rulings that regard the ethics of war as an important part of *jihad.* It is safe to say that the modern radical appropriation of *jihad* interprets it so as to say the cause justifies anything and everything in the way of conduct.

This reflects a larger problem: while classical thinkers focused attention on *jus in bello*, the focus of modern writers, on the other hand, is on *jus ad bellum*, with little attention to the conduct of war once begun. As John Kelsay argues, "The momentum of Islamic thinking about justice

at other times internal enemies of the Muslim state. The use of the word *jihad* for these wars of national liberation or internal rebellion among Muslim nations raises serious questions about the inappropriate use of religiously sanctioned *jihad*; and even more serious questions can be raised about its proclamation by one Muslim state warring against another, as with Iraq and Iran two decades ago.

[7] The last Caliph (whose role even then was only nominal) was deposed by Kemal Ataturk in 1923.

and war leads to an emphasis on such *jus ad bellum* concerns as right authority and just cause, and ultimately to a discussion of how conceptions of nature and the destiny of human beings set a framework for discussions of war."[8] This overemphasis on the *jus ad bellum* criteria at the expense of the *jus in bello* criteria—which formed the major focus of the classic discussions of *jihad* and served to guide wars fought to advance Muslim hegemony—has served to justify even the use of terrorism and individual acts of violence against those deemed "the enemy." Today, *jihad* as a divinely sanctioned means to combat the enemy often provides little more than a carte-blanche justification for going to war for reasons of realpolitik without concern for limitations upon the means.

Thus it is that the term *jihad*, with its long and complex history in Islam as it interacted with political power, has come to be used and abused to justify the seemingly endless violence plaguing many countries in the Middle East and elsewhere. The frequent abuse of the term by religious leaders has led many Western observers to treat *jihad* essentially in the meaning of "holy war," with an implication that Muslim international relations will continue to be conflict-ridden because, as a religious obligation to fight dark forces of disbelief and arrogance (*harb al-kuffar*), *jihad* will continue to determine Muslim relations with the non-Muslim world. But *jihad* has also been used to speak about conflict among the "brother nation-states" in the "family" (*al-bughat*), and certainly this *jihad* is not the same as the one fought against non-Muslims.[9]

To add to this complexity, we should note the historically entrenched depiction of wars between Muslims and the Christian world which continue to loom large in Western understanding of *jihad*. Most Western attempts to explain the culture of violence in the Muslim world have connected this culture to the religious appropriation of the term *jihad* in the meaning of "holy war" and as such to a Muslim political goal of extending "the sphere of Islam" (*dar al-islam*), that is, territories administered by the Muslim state, by obliterating "the sphere of war" (*dar al-harb*), that is, territories to be subdued. The two phrases, as argued by these writers, highlight the theological foundation of Muslim religious convictions about forming a Muslim empire that must ultimately subdue and dominate the non-Muslim world. Such an evaluation of *jihad* is based entirely on decon-

---

8 John Kelsay, *Bosnia and the Muslim Critique of Modernity, in* RELIGION AND JUSTICE IN THE WAR OVER BOSNIA 120 (G. Scott Davis, ed., 1999).

9 Muslim jurists treat insurgency warfare in terms of rebellion by Muslims living under an Islamic order. *Ahkam al-Bughat* delineate laws that regulate the treatment of those who rebel against the ruler of the Islamic state. These rules deal with the treatment of political and religious dissidents. *See* Khaled Abu El Fadl, Ahkam al-Bughat: *Irregular Warfare and the Law of Rebellion in Islam, in* CROSS, CRESCENT, AND SWORD: THE JUSTIFICATION AND LIMITATION OF WAR IN WESTERN AND ISLAMIC TRADITION 149–176 (James T. Johnson & John Kelsay eds., 1990).

textualized readings of a narrow range of theological-juridical sources.[10] The theological-juridical expression of the doctrine and the legal issues surrounding *jihad*, as well as modern interpretations required by such momentous changes for the Muslim world as colonialism and responses to modernity and the West, require us to be cautious in linking the past heritage to contemporary Muslim responses to oppression and aggression by Muslim and non-Muslim forces.

Nevertheless, with the growing influence of the religious extremism in the last three decades, it is possible to speak about the influence of a major article of faith in dealing with unjust rulers on the on-going conflicts in the Muslim world, whether that conflict involves non-Muslim countries or Muslim countries with illegitimate rulers in power. This is the belief that the rulers of these countries are perceived as the followers of the pre-Islamic system of the *jahiliyya*—the period that is regarded as ungodly by these ultra-pious Muslims.[11] More deeply, this belief reflects an even deeper one, one that can be exploited to generate perpetual conflict: namely, belief in the absolute superiority of Islam, belief that regards it as the final and perfected message that abrogated the pre-Qur'anic religions like Judaism and Christianity. This sense of spiritual-moral superiority not only serves to instigate interfaith conflicts, it also provides sufficient religiously crafted justifications for the mutual condemnation of, and ensuing deadly conflict in, the intra-faith relations between Sunnites and Shi'ites. Before going on I must talk about this common conviction.

"THE PERFECT RELIGION THAT WILL REPLACE ALL OTHER RELIGIONS"

The debate over the role of religious ideas in engendering deadly conflicts around the globe continues endlessly. Yet I believe that the importance of religious beliefs in spawning conflicts among the "peoples of the Book" cannot be underestimated. In the Islamic context, my own observations lead me to affirm that religion and religious beliefs are a source of much activism, for good and ill, in the Muslim world. During the most recent conflicts, such as in Bosnia and Chechnya, the statements calling the people for *jihad* make frequent references about the world in

---

[10] For an analysis of this *see* EDWARD SAID, COVERING ISLAM (1999); for an example, *see* SAMUEL HUNTINGTON, THE CLASH OF CIVILIZATIONS (1996).

[11] The term *jahiliyya* to describe the rule under an unjust ruler or a believer who does not follow the Islamic law in administering the affairs of the community appears in the "creed" of the extremists around the Muslim world. In THE NEGLECTED DUTY: THE CREED OF SADAT'S ASSASSINS AND ISLAMIC RESURGENCE IN THE MIDDLE EAST, Johannes J. G. Jansen has translated this creed. In the section entitled *The Comparison between the Mongols and Today's Rulers*, *id.* at 172–75, the author cites the Qur'an and early jurists regarding the mode of governance based on the un-Islamic world (*jahiliyya*) and declares war against such a system as religiously obligatory.

which Muslims are increasingly under physical threat by non-Muslim governments and groups. Anti-modernism is prominent in the religious pronouncements. Closely related to discourses against modernity are theological arguments against the West, the U.S. in particular.

The source of many a deadly conflict for and among Muslims has been the belief that Islam is the only true religion that will dominate all other religions, superseding them. Such religious exclusivism rules out the plurality of faiths and communities and ensuing toleration founded upon the principle of co-existence. It effectively rules out peaceful co-existence among different faith communities, and within the community itself. The establishment of institutes for *Dar al-taqrib bayna al-madhahib* (Reconciliation between various schools of thought) in Cairo, Egypt and Qumm, Iran have a single goal in mind: to understand the differences between various Muslim schools of thought, and generate a meaningful dialogue between the majority Sunnites and the minority Shi'ites. However, the extremists on both sides regard these attempts to reconcile the Shi'ites and the Sunnites as nothing less than a compromise on one's monopoly over the religious truth. When this exclusivist doctrine governs interfaith relations, then it has the potential to disrupt peaceful relations between different faith communities. Consequently, it is important to examine in some detail the idea of the perfect religion abrogating all other religions—the idea that can be retrieved by the extremists in any tradition to dehumanize the religious "other."

The idea that Islam is the ultimate and perfect religion in the line of Abrahamic religions is derived from the Tradition (the *Sunna*). Indeed, one might even suggest that the idea of Islam being the only monotheistic tradition that offers the indubitable guarantee of salvation in the hereafter is *post-Qur'anic.* For the Qur'an saw itself as confirming rather than altering the central message of the Abrahamic religions that preceded it chronologically. More importantly, it saw itself as a conclusive revelation in the ongoing process of divine guidance from the day the earth became inhabited by the first human couple, Adam and Eve. Consequently, the Qur'an does not take up the issue of the abrogation or supersession[12] of the previous Abrahamic religions of Christianity or Judaism and prescribe the forced conversion of the followers of these religions. Quite to the contrary, it recognizes the salvific efficacy of the Abrahamic faiths, whose central doctrines Islam understands itself to share.

---

[12] I am using the word "supersession" in the meaning of *naskh al-shara,* and not in the meaning of abrogation of the entire pre-Qur'anic revelation received by Moses or Jesus. This latter notion is not supported at all in the Qur'an. Muslim scholars are also aware of the fact that it is *naskh al-shara* of Moses and Jesus that is their point of polemical reference, and not the *wahy* received by these Abrahamic prophets prior to the revelation of the Qur'an.

In the light of growing tensions in inter- and intra-faith relations in countries like Sudan, Pakistan and Afghanistan, an extremely important question needs to be raised about the way religions respond to the plurality of human responses to the religious impulse. How does a religion treat those who do not share its salvation narrative? The question should also lead us to explore the ways in which a society's public space is subtly shaped, and sometimes directly controlled, by the dominant faith community. Furthermore, and most importantly for our purposes, it should reveal the strategies that were adopted in Islam to regulate legal-ethical relations with its non-Muslim minorities at home, and to maintain international relations abroad.

The theological-juridical justifications for *jihad* against non-Muslims that were provided by the Muslim jurists who had hoped that the entire world would become the "sphere of Islam" render complex and difficult, though not impossible, forging of alliances or collaborations, at least temporary ones, between Islamic and non-Islamic states. Are there resources within Islam that allow or encourage, and then guide, such inter-religious alliances or collaborations? Given the realities of globalization, and the growing recognition of the inevitably international shape of most difficulties the international community faces today, it seems that such collaborations will be increasingly necessary. Can Islam find the internal resources to permit and encourage them? Indeed it can; Islamic law has the capacity to legitimate, at least partially, the "public" international order and its requirements, in ways that go beyond the classical formulations of exclusively religious membership of the Islamic nation-states in Muslim organizations.[13]

A good example of what I mean may be found in the debates occupying this volume, namely the debates concerning the possibilities of international, inter-traditional humanitarian intervention. It is religiously possible to speak of humanitarian intervention in protecting the lives and property of non-Muslims living in Muslim countries. Political and religious leaders may be resentful of non-Muslim involvement in such interventions, but they might grudgingly accept such intervention, and the presence of non-Muslims in them, as potentially already sanctioned by the tradition of the Prophet: "I will take up the case of people who are under my protection (the *dhimmis*) on the day of judgment if they are ill-treated by my people."[14] This tradition provides the rudiments of a way to legitimate humanitarian intervention, although it needs serious development, and attention not only to the religious justification for such intervention but to its political acceptability, especially when the "oppressors" are Muslim.

---

13 *See* THE ISLAMIC ROOTS OF DEMOCRATIC PLURALISM, *supra* note 1.

14 *Id.* at Ch. 3.

THE CRISIS OF INTERPRETING ISLAMIC *JIHAD* FOR WORLD PEACE

It is appropriate to speak about a crisis of retrieval and interpretation of the rulings about *jihad* today. In the world of nation-states where international relations are conducted without any reference to religious affiliation (or lack thereof) of the member states, the discourse about *jihad* among the extremist groups gives rise to uncompromising attitudes that render all chances of negotiated peace practically impossible. The crisis created by the selective retrieval of past rulings on *jihad*, and their interpretation by the leaders of radical movements—leaders who lack the necessary training in contextualizing the past rulings to investigate their applicability in modern times—is a serious one, which has led to untold misery suffered by the innocent civilians caught in the crossfire.

Traditionally, there are three basic steps that Muslim jurists must take in order to derive fresh rulings on the subject of how Islamic nations should relate to the "sphere of war" today:

1. Investigation into the *usul*, the fundamental sources like the Qur'an and the Sunna (the Tradition) that provide direct or indirect statements describing or defining the "sphere of war" and its limits;
2. Investigation of the *furu*, the paradigm cases that guide jurists in determining the legal-ethical outcome of a given present case;
3. Investigation of the *mawdu'at*, "objects" or "situations" that might be analogous to paradigm cases, in order to understand the changed context and the relevant ordinances to decide whether the "sphere of war" today can be described the same way as it was in the past.

The *ahkam*—rulings—can be derived only after the above three steps in the investigation have been followed.

This traditional method of deriving fresh decisions has given rise to several fundamental problems related to the determination of the "situational" context of *jihad* against both Muslim rebels and non-Muslims. First of all, it is obvious to the jurists in the traditional centers (who are severely criticized by the radicals) that Muslims are not living under the universal caliphal state. Therefore, the legal terms used to divide the world between *dar al-islam* and *dar al-harb* are defunct in modern times. In fact, the use of *dar al-islam* for any Muslim country is legally problematic. Moreover, during the Iran-Iraq conflict and the Gulf War, Muslim countries were pitted against one another, and neither of these wars could be described in terms of *jihad*, because in both cases the rhetorical use of *jihad* had rendered the term meaningless. Hence, the classical rulings and the terminology used there proved to be largely irrelevant in using the idea of *jihad* in contemporary international affairs. The requirement to investigate the changed situation prior to issuing a legal decision affecting the status of Muslim countries under consideration remains contentious even now. The role of Muslim jurists in ascertaining the legality of *jihad* in the "Family" is circumvented by the realities of public international order where Islam is no longer a determining factor in resolving the conflict peacefully. Neither the classical heritage nor the contemporary radical interpretations of *jihad* have proven able to provide solutions to the concerns for peace among ordinary Muslim peoples in the Muslim nations.

Islamic legal inquiry always emphasized the necessity for individual rational inquiry regarding the situational context in which one exists; and this commitment always entailed that people should be involved in representing their own concerns in all matters related to their social and political well-being. Implicit in this pre-requisite is the assumption that any legal decision affecting not only Muslims but also non-Muslim minorities living within Muslim territories should be made while allowing the people to exercise their right to determine their general well-being in the society. But, in fact, the granting of the protected religious minority (*ahl al-dhimma*) status by the law, which accorded autonomous legal status to the minority, was deduced from an ideological standpoint of the superiority of the Muslim community. There was no acknowledgement of the Qur'anic monotheistic egalitarianism in dealing with the Christians and the Jews of the empire. Lurking behind the concept of the *ahl al-dhimma* was the supersessionist theology of the Muslim scholars in which the only correct form of monotheism was the religion of Islam. Moreover, because of this theological conviction, the institutional recognition of these subject peoples as spiritually and morally inferior became one of the major factors in obstructing the integrating objects and situations that would have gradually led to the creation of an egalitarian civil society in the Muslim world. Of course, the majority of the discriminatory rulings against non-Muslims, it must be pointed out, were derived by reference to the juristic principle that "averting causes of corruption has precedence over bringing about that which has benefit" (*dar'u al-mafasid muqaddam ala jalb al-masalih*).[15] This and other similar juristic principles were designed to regulate inter-human relationships in the law, but were more often than not invoked to curb the rights of minorities to function as full citizens in Muslim societies.

The supersessionist theology notwithstanding, a cursory glance at the juridical decisions made in relation to the followers of other monotheistic faiths indicates that, relatively speaking, Muslim jurists succeeded in pursuing the Qur'anic impulse towards asserting individual rights of all the followers of the Abrahamic traditions on the basis of God-centered equal-

---

[15] This principle has been widely used to curb women's rights in Muslim society. See, for instance, MUHAMMAD AL-GHAZALI, QADAYA AL-MAR'A' BAYNA AL-TAQALID AL-RAKIDA WA AL-WAFIDA (1992), on several occasions justifies certain traditional stances on woman's status by referring to this principle.

ity—not infrequently more profoundly than did Christians.[16] And, although Muslims retained wide authority in the society, laws were enacted to give minorities unprecedented respect and protection in the Muslim polity.

CONCLUDING REMARKS

The views expressed here are not necessarily shared by all Muslims. These matters, and the positions put forward here, are loudly discussed and contested in Egypt, Iran and other Middle Eastern countries. Yet I believe that there is an emerging consensus regarding these matters, and I have tried to show how such a consensus could be encouraged and nurtured in ways which would provide real usefulness in constructing a distinctly Islamic rationale for humanitiarian intervention.[17]

Let me conclude by underscoring that the deep issue to be worked out now is precisely the ultimate character of Islamic religious exclusivism, and how that is manifest in Muslim's work on *jihad. Kitab al-jihad* (The Book on *Jihad*) section of the juridical corpus continues to exercise enormous influence in the way the Muslim world conceives its relation with the non-Muslim "other." One can hardly ignore the influence that the religious statements contained in the legal rulings and the widely circulated traditions have in the formulation of policies affecting Muslim non-Muslim relations. In any work on Islamic law *Kitab al-jihad* is a key to our understanding of the way in which the Muslim community related itself to the world at large, including to the tolerated minorities within its own borders. If anything, it is the rationalization of *jihad* in the jurisprudence that demonstrates the interaction between theology and politics in its most clear contours.

In the final analysis, no comprehension of Christian-Muslim or Jewish-Muslim relations is possible without adequate understanding of the theology of supersession and its impact upon the Muslim treatment of its religious minorities. Recognition of religious pluralism in Islam has always been determined either by the absolutist or the relativist claim that Islam is the "only" accepted way. And it is the Muslim jurists who have allowed one or the other interpretation to prevail, depending on their evaluation of the perceived threat to Islam and its peoples. Only if present trends in the world are seen as supportive of the true nature of Islam are Muslims likely to accept religious pluralism in their own countries, much less to intervene on behalf of non-Muslims elsewhere who are being persecuted by civil of religious authorities.

---

16 *See* THE ISLAMIC ROOTS OF DEMOCRATIC PLURALISM, *supra* note 1, Ch. 2.

17 I have cited a number of sources in my ISLANIC ROOTS OF DEMOCRATIC PLURALISM to show the emerging consensus among Muslims on these issues. *See also* the works by Khalid Abu El-Fadl cited *supra*.

CHAPTER 3

AN ETHIC OF HUMANITARIAN INTERVENTION: A POST-SEPTEMBER 11 PERSPECTIVE

*Donald W. Shriver, Jr.**

THE OTHER FACE OF WAR

In an October 14, 2001, review of two new books on international terrorism, Robert D. Kaplan began by observing that terrorism "is a diseased variant of modern, total war that had its debut in 1864 when President Abraham Lincoln and his generals reluctantly targeted the farms, homes and factories of Southern civilians in an effort to bring a swift end to the Civil War." And he ended with the view:

> Realism thrives during times when people feel insecure, just as idealism does during times when security is taken for granted. The post-cold-war era, a 12-year hiatus from the collapse of the Berlin wall to the collapse of the World Trade Center, saw a burgeoning humanitarianism toward the Balkans and Africa. But that age is now over. . . .[1]

Kaplan might have carried further his comparison of the 1864 and post-September 11 events, however, with some expansion into the subsequent history: how, after 1865, for the next eleven years, the federal government pursued a policy dubbed "reconstruction," and how, as he wrote, the United States was preparing to pound Afghanistan with bombs and food. The bombs are meant to prepare the way for changes of political power in that country; the food, to sustain the life of civilians deemed to be innocent of the evils of their current government. In both of these two very different historical contexts, a government wages a war with a peace in view. And in both, there is the intention to restore a post-war society in conformity with the political preferences of the victor.

---

* President Emeritus, Union Theological Seminary in New York.

1 *The Faceless Enemy*, THE NEW YORK TIMES BOOK REVIEW, 11 (Oct. 14, 2001).

In post-September 11 retrospect, Americans have been reminded that in the early 1990s our government aided the anti-Soviet forces and helped install them in power, only to deny them American economic or other aid. A devastated Afghanistan was left to its own devices while a commitment to "nation-building" went forward in Bosnia, Serbia, and Kosovo. One can only speculate on how the newly defeated Confederate States of America might have "reconstructed" themselves if left on their own after 1865, or how Afghanistan might have taken a different political course if the United States and other Western nations had risen to the challenge of post-1993 economic help to that devastated country.[2]

We may not call it "burgeoning humanitarianism," but the fact remains that something resembling social-political reconstruction is still an element in any conceivably prudent political aim of warmakers in modern global society. Nobody these harried days in America seems about to suggest that, this time around, the Western world should leave the Afghans in their poverty, now that their Taliban government has gone down in military defeat. Indeed, the sense that, after 1993, the West should have undertaken a serious economic development program for the Afghans has a like analogy in the reflection that after 1865 the victorious North never did undertake serious economic development for defeated Southerners white or black—especially black. The legacy of that neglect extended deep into the 20th century.

In short, the notion of "humanitarian intervention," as an actual or a desirable sequel to armed warfare, is not really so new or so dispensable from the policy plans of international warmakers and peacemakers as Kaplan may think. The "long war" which an American president is currently calling us to undertake against terrorism has to entail a longer war against all the reasons why defeated enemies might seek to fight again. If there is one stable bit of political wisdom that the 20th century history of war has to offer to the world of the 21st, it is the contrast between the Versailles Treaty and the Marshall Plan: vengeance doesn't work in international political affairs. Neither does leaving a defeated people to their own devices.

This is, in effect, an updating of Augustine's injunction that war should be waged so as to insure both peace and "just policy." Such a policy is perhaps even more necessary in today's complex and divided world than it was in the Roman Empire of the fifth century—and takes

---

[2] In the case of the South, one does not really have to rely on speculation. After 1876, with the demise of the federal attempts to "reconstruct" relations between newly freed slaves and the white majority and with the freedom of the white majority to re-install repression of black citizen rights, one of the goals of the war was speedily frustrated. It would largely remain so for a century.

very different forms. Thus, both an understanding of the ends sought and an appreciation of the means to those ends is an essential part of Christian thinking about conflict.

Just War in Christian Thinking

As Professor Johnson indicates in his review of views about war held by various Christian churches, these fall into three clusters:

- Those which reject the use of armed force as one of the aspects of life in this sinful world, from which they seek to withdraw;
- Those who hold, with Dante and other political philosophers, that peace can be achieved only by establishing the kingdom of God on earth, which in practice requires a just political order superior to all states, who will relinquish the right to use force.
- The "just war" tradition, in which the goal of establishing a just peace is one of the pre-conditions for the utlization of force, along with acknowledgement and acceptance of restrictions on the way in which it is employed.

The Presbyterian church, along with the majority of Catholics and Protestants, has often affirmed the "just war" ethic first formulated by St. Augustine in the fifth century. The concept focuses on the two questions of when war is justified and how war can be justly conducted. Like any robust ethical criteria, just war thinking limits as well as legitimizes the role of violence in society. The ethic means to cut both ways—when not to go to war and how not to conduct war as well as when and how to do so.

Significant in the history of this ethic is its largely secular verbal expression, which—especially since the wars of religion in 17th century Europe—avoids the implication that Almighty God endorses and backs human military might. If the ethic excludes pacifism, it also excludes the crusade.

The elements of the just war ethic are well known:

Just reasons for going to war (*jus ad bellum*):

- A just intention on the part of the warmakers, especially the intention to reestablish peace.
- A just cause, *e.g.*, defending one's nation against foreign invasion.
- A cause *more* just than the partially just cause of the enemy, *e.g.*, the latter's quest for economic security by invading other countries.
- Authorization of the war by a legitimate authority, *i.e.*, a government.
- A likelihood of military success.
- The resort to war after all other possible steps of prevention have been tried.

Two principles for the just conduct of war (*jus in bello*):

- Proportionality: only so much destruction of life and property as is necessary to serve the just intention and the just cause.
- Discrimination: between military and civilian targets.

Measured between these principles, the wars of U.S. history will not all be judged as clearly "just" in honest retrospect. The Mexican War of 1845 was as much an attack on Mexico as it was defensive of the United States. The Spanish-American War had its imperialistic aims, and among the ambiguities of the Vietnam War were questions about "likelihood of military success" without violations of proportionality and discrimination. Perhaps the most colossal abandonment of *in bello* principles of just war, however, occurred in this and other countries' conduct of World War II. By its end city-bombing became routine, climaxed by the weapon used against Hiroshima and Nagasaki. We have yet to learn how discriminating the bombs in Afghanistan will turn out to have been, though American commanders there have stressed that modern bombs are uniquely capable of missing civilians while hitting military targets. In any event, it remains practically as well as ethically mandatory that, if warmakers are responsible for helping to rebuild societies after a war's end, they must seek to limit the damage to essential components of those societies while war is waged. Thus, the commander may have to reconcile the wisdom of knocking out military targets such as bridges, a measure which will disrupt traffic after the war as well as during it or of destroying electric power plants, which will slow the productions of armaments during war and of essential civilian goods after the war is over. Moreover, even well-directed attacks on barracks, supply dumps, troop concentrations, airfields, etc., can cause extensive collateral damage to surrounding housing, schools and shops with the doubly undesirable consequences of causing heavy casualties and undermining civil society.[3] Thus, as Dr. Pierce would doubtless agree, there is a tension between the military objective of winning the war as quickly as possible, and with the fewest possible deaths among the members of the armed services, and the moral objective of limiting the destruction of life and property—which, if we look to the post-war world, is also a national objective.

The just war ethic applies not only to waging war but also to deciding whether to wage it. First and foremost among the factors which should influence that division is a "just intention . . . , especially the intention to reestablish peace." As has been urged previously, that peace should be one which ultimately enables all participants to function effectively

---

[3] The reader may have in mind his own examples: mine include the Navy Yard in Norfolk, Virginia, headquarters of the U.S. Atlantic Fleet, and Andrews Air Force Base, just outside of Washington, DC. Though perhaps the Pentagon would be a better illustration!

and to provide their citizens with at least the minimum requirements for food, shelter, educations, medical care, etc. More importantly, it should enable those citizens to participate in the formation of national policy, in the expectation that this will strengthen the forces promoting peace and freedom. And while we should not expect a nation in the heat of anger and the flush of determination to frame political objectives which many would see as favoring the enemy, we can ask that it not endorse Draconian proposals for punishing that enemy[4]—thereby insuring that it will forever remain one.

Preventive Intervention

A second bit of correlative wisdom is that intervention by one political power into the internal affairs of another, may on occasion, be warranted. In retrospect, this certainly applies to Hitlerian Germany, especially after the revelations of the Nazi genocides and the horrors of Auschwitz and its kindred camps across Nazi-occupied Europe. Had the moral slumber of France, Britain, and the United States not been so laced with both ignorance and fear of the Nazi menace, the war might have come sooner, been shorter, and served humanity better.

This is equally true in today's world, and holds with regard to conflicts within states as well as those between states. Indeed, during the past two decades the former have been both bloodier and more frequent than the latter, with perhaps a million people being killed in Cambodia and over half a million in Rwanda.

Not to be forgotten in this context is the conviction of United Nations General Romeo Delaire that with 5,000 outside troops he could have quelled the Rwandan massacre. When President Clinton apologized for the inaction of the UN and the West in this tragedy, he belatedly put his own country on notice that preventive action may now be the strategy of choice for nations that oppose "crimes against humanity," whatever their nature and their origin.

There are, regrettably, a number of factors inhibiting preventive action. One is the opposition by many former colonies in Africa and Asia to anything that might infringe on their hard-won sovereignty. Another is that the UN Charter is focused almost entirely on coping with aggression by one state against another and lumps internal conflicts and other undefined "threats to international peace and security" under Article 51

---

4 This was the path that the United States took in WW II. Briefly, in 1944, Allied leaders considered the proposal by U.S. Treasury Secretary Robert Morgenthau that Germany be returned to its 18th century "agricultural and pastoral" economy. War Secretary Henry Stimson countered: "Such methods do not prevent war, they breed it." Roosevelt and Churchill came to agree with Stimson. *Cf.* my discussion in AN ETHIC FOR ENEMIES: FORGIVENESS IN POLITICS 79 (1995).

whose application requires positive action by the UN Security Council.[5] A third is that many states adhere in practice to the "realist" school of international relations which argues that a resort to arms is warranted when—and only when—national interests are threatened, with the magnitude of the effort roughly proportional to the importance of the interests at stake.

This "realist" tradition says that genocide in Rwanda had no direct impact on the interests of nations outside of Africa. Therefore, Western inaction to that event in 1994 was more justifiable than inaction in the case of Bosnia, which is neighbor to Western Europe. In a world already interconnected by sinews of economy and communication, however, there is something ironically idealistic about this version of realism. No one knows yet what may be the evil fruit of a Rwandan memory of 1994 as a time when outside help might have cut short their internal rampage of murder, just as no one knows exactly which neglects of the interests of Islamic peoples have fueled their various resentments of the West. Americans now tell each other that their "world has changed" from secure to insecure; but only the naive would claim that, prior to September 11, the interests of Americans could not be shaken by other interests in the world. Two world wars and the Cold War taught us one side of our vulnerability to power remote from our shores. It now turns out that technology, like money, is "fungible" for the doing of either good or evil around the planet. It is now possible for a small group of people to inflict so much evil on so many others that one does not have to be a naive idealist to counter so-called realism with the thought: Ought some nations intervene in the affairs of other nations for mutual good?

There would seem to be no reasonable alternative. A desire that the world's peoples return to letting each other alone will be an impossible dream in the year 2002. Equally impossible—and unacceptable—is the desire in dealing with each other that we do so only by utilizing our potentials for doing evil to each other. It may now be impossible to separate, on a world scale, the expansion of our ability to hurt each other from the expansion of our ability to help. All of this is to say that the day of *in*humane intervention is so little over that its very intensification in the terrorist threat requires that the day of humane intervention *not* be over.

Political policymakers now need, and need desperately, some new combinations of self-interested and other-interested perspectives on the empirical and moral dimensions of world conflict. Old in ethical theorizing of the West is the alleged conflict of human action based on good benefit versus action based on right principle. The interconnected world of nations in this new century presents a complex challenge to conceiv-

---

[5] For Further discussion of this point, *see* Johnson, James T. "The Law of Nations: Religion, Ethics and International Law Bearing on Conflict and Peace."

ing self-interest and other-interest as interdependent. It is as if the 21st century at last offers empirical proof of the pertinence of John Donne's great principle: "No man is an island . . . ," for the interests of people living in seemingly remote regions of the world really are now closely tied to the interests of all humanity. Why else would Americans be suddenly aware of how a poor, remote country called Afghanistan may be deeply implicated in our lives and our deaths anywhere in our fifty states?

The 1990s may well have been a kindly window on the world for most Americans and Europeans, leading us to aspire prematurely to playing the role of peacemakers and peacekeepers in the Middle East, India and Pakistan, Sri Lanka, and the Balkans. The experience of that decade suggests the limits as well as the scope of American and Western power for bringing peace to the rest of the world. But it also suggests the need for settling small wars before they grow into large ones. Thus, none of us, including Robert Kaplan, should take lightly the signs of a new determination among a uniquely large cluster of countries, precisely in the 1990s, to forge institutional alternatives for settling human conflict worldwide—measures which would include relief and reconstruction and international law courts as well as the interposition of armed forces between combatants.

No one knows what may be the eventual outcomes of outside intervention in the Balkans over the past decade, but it would be blind to conclude, after so few years, that UN peacekeepers have saved no significant number of lives there or had no role in the promise of significant political change in Serbia, Kosovo, and Bosnia. Those years are a part of what Elazar Barkan describes as the hopeful stumbling of the world towards "a new threshold of morality in international politics." International refusal to intervene in the genocides of Biafra and Cambodia left a residue of shared guilt among many political leaders and publics. The establishment of war crime tribunals for Rwanda and the former Yugoslavia express something of this guilt; and, says Barkan, the ultimate military actions of the West in Bosnia and Kosovo were largely justified in moral, not *realpolitik* terms. "In large measure it was a response to the growing moral fervor in international politic and the fear of today's leaders of doing nothing in the face of mass human disaster." The list of consensual agreement on moral principle here is short. Few Western leaders have spoken of absolute justice. But some new beginnings of international law are underfoot, says Barkan. Post-modernist relativism has its insights, but there are some agreements on moral principle that humans worldwide will have to reach, if we are to keep our potentials for murder at bay.[6]

---

6 *Cf.* ELAZAR BARKAN, THE GUILT OF NATIONS: RESTITUTION AND NEGOTIATING HISTORICAL INJUSTICES (2000). *Cf. id.* at xviii, xxxii, and xxxvi–vii.

FROM JUST WAR TO JUST PEACE: ONE CHURCH-RELATED EFFORT TO IDENTIFY THE CRITERIA

Among other agencies which have reason to think about the complex issues at stake in this matter have been the Christian churches of the United States. Here I want to review the effort of just one denomination, the Presbyterian Church (U.S.A.), to explore the concept of humanitarian, international intervention under the rubric of "just peacemaking." As the authors of the 1998 Presbyterian resolution concede, humanitarian intervention, like war itself, is a messy project that easily tempts its leaders to leave the discussion of ethics to non-combatants. Nonetheless, they observed, modern war and modern peace require some new, expanded definitions of justice if military force is to contribute to the classical war-aim of peace. Both the failures of intervention—*e.g.*, Somalia in 1993 and Rwanda in 1994—and the limited successes—*e.g.*, Bosnia in 1996 and Kosovo in 1999—offer positive and negative wisdom for elaborating the just war ethic into a new version, which these scholars called "Just Peacemaking and the Call for International Intervention for Humanitarian Rescue."

As passed by the General Assembly of the church in 1998, the core claims of the resolution are seven. Some of these principles are slight modifications of the traditional just war ethic. Others are relatively new specifications. All confront formidable empirical-historical difficulties for concrete implementation by policymakers considering intervention. Something basic about the role of ethics in human societies has to be remembered here as in every consideration of the relation of the "real" to the "ideal": a principle may get eroded by circumstance but is not thereby invalidated. Violated in one circumstance, a good principle needs to be preserved against the day when it will be needed again—and this time heeded.

Below I want briefly to review each of the seven Presbyterian-crafted guidelines for humanitarian intervention with brief references to both the success and failure of intervention in the past few years, up to and including the current American response to the terrorism of September 11. As will be evident in my commentaries, I can personally affirm these principles along with reservations. Like norms in general, these are terms for deliberation more than detailed instructions for action.

1. *Intervention must respond to a real and genuine need that cannot be met by other means.* This is a revision of the "last resort" rule of the just war tradition. The United Nations Charter mandates only two situations that justify proposals for intervention that come to its Security Council—invasion across national borders and genocide. There is empirical tension between these two measures of "genuine need." For Barkan and numerous others, mass murder inside the borders of one country should be an

occasion of *protective* invasion by other countries. Sovereignty in this situation must be violated if lives are to be saved.

Notoriously in the Rwandan case, many advocates of intervention believed (with UN commander Romeo Delaire) that an outside force could have stalled the massacre if deployed before or at the beginning of the killing. The U.S. State Department and the Pentagon, smarting from the failures of the 1993 intervention in Somalia and fearful of American public reaction to a new adventure in Central Africa, opted to do nothing. When finally the U.N. Security Council authorized a force of 5,500 troops, four months after Delaire's warnings of the impending event, it was too late. Vice Secretary-General Kofi Annan expressed his own anguish at this international blind eye turned toward a tragedy which, if any event ever did, embodied the "genuine need" which the Presbyterians have in mind here:

> Nobody should feel he has a clear conscience in this business. If the picture of tens of thousands of human bodies rotting and gnawed on by the dogs . . . do not wake us up out of our apathy, I don't know what will.[7]

Single nations and all nations together do not always have the capacity, not to speak of the will, to respond to genuine needs everywhere; but Rwanda is probably the best single recent example of international failure to intervene when the capacity was there without the will. Perhaps the most embarrassing possible factor in this failure was the lack of resonance, especially in the American and European publics, for saving lives in Africa as compared to the same in the Balkans. Not just difficult logistics but implicit racism may have contributed to that blinding of Western eyes.

2. *Intervention must have a reasonable chance of alleviating the crisis it seeks to overcome.* "Reasonable" means military and political prudence. The major difference here from the "success" norm of *jus ad bellam* is the prominence of the forward-looking political element in the prudent calculus. Like all consequential ethics, predictions of future results are always problematic, and debates over "reasonable chances of success" can never avoid the uncertainties of all resorts to organized violence. Whether in the hills of Rwanda or the mountains of Afghanistan, military judgments and political aims must qualify each other; and this means that political leaders, military strategists, and publics at large deserve debate and deliberation over the risks of intervening and not intervening. And reading the results of one intervention can make a great difference in conceiving

---

7 Quoted from LE MONDE, May 25, 1994, by GERARD PRUNIER, THE RWANDA CRISIS: HISTORY OF A GENOCIDE, 276 (1995–97).

another. In 1995, belatedly but decisively, NATO bombs brought a halt to Serbian war in Bosnia, and few observers afterwards would deny that UN troops in Bosnia and Kosovo are still necessary for maintaining peace there. Bosnia currently is "off the screen" for much of the world media, but that is because the slow rebuilding of that society goes ahead now with large international help.

3. *It must constitute humanitarian rescue and not cloak the pursuit of the economic or narrow security interests of the intervening powers.* Instances of "pure" humanitarian rescue by outside powers are rare, and when associated with some economic or other security interests, the humanitarian argument has reinforcing allies, as was the case, for example, in the Gulf War of 1991. There, the UN Security Council acted on a clear case of violation of Kuwait's borders by invading Iraqis. But as everyone knows, oil was at stake in this conflict; and half a million soldiers were mobilized to protect its supply to Europe and America. The case of Rwanda was radically different. Contrary to General Dellaire and UN Secretary Kofi Annan, defenders of the realist tradition would say that no economic or political interest should have brought American and European soldiers to Rwanda in early 1994. Is there ever a case for saving the lives of people in another country at some cost of lives in one's own? Somalia in 1993 seemed to offer an opportunity to say "yes" to this question, but the actual loss of American lives there dimmed the courage of an American president for undertaking similar risks in the spring of 1994 in Rwanda.

Collective international action in the name of this principle has much political history against it, but it is worth noting that retrospective blame—including the actions of international courts—is no substitute for a prospective commitment to the prevention of mass murder wherever it is about to occur. There are *levels* of unjust violence that compel outside preventive action whether or not clear material interests are at stake for the outsiders. Interests are not likely to disappear in calculations of international cooperation, but defenders of humanitarian intervention in the 21st century will want to remember that short-sighted definitions of "national interest" led the United States to abandon the League of Nations in 1920 and Britain to abandon Czechoslovakia in 1938, only to lead them into a war that, it turned out, challenged all their interests, ideal and material. "Self-interest" may be a concept applicable to collections of people, but a lot depends on what sort of self the collection is interested in.[8]

---

[8] The sociologist Max Weber coined the distinction between "ideal" and "material" interest. After September 11, 2001, Americans woke up to their material interest in Afghanistan, but to be remembered is the sympathy for the plight of Muslims in Bosnia and Kosovo that finally stirred American and European leaders to military action in both those countries. This fact bolsters the current claim of the American government that it is not the enemy of Islam. Humanitarian interest can end up serving material interest, just as mate-

4. *Intervention, whenever possible, should have international auspices in order to achieve the greatest presumption of legitimacy.* In the early months of 2001, the new Bush administration openly challenged this principle. Then, suddenly with September 11, it woke up to the fact that humanitarian rescue in the United States, too, requires international collaboration. The irony here is that a terrorist network by definition is a "transnational" organization as is much of the contemporary world economy, the former making full use of the latter for its anti-humanitarian aims. Having promoted economic globalization with ideological fervor, this administration, one presumes, would be much alarmed if it discovered that no other world leaders are willing to label terrorism a crime or to collaborate in combating it. Classic just war doctrine has been used mostly in questions of whether a nation should go to war or not, typically for self-defense. But the assumption behind principle 4 is that ethical justification is the more likely the larger the world consensus. This takes seriously claims like Barkan's that a minimal but indispensable world political ethic is in the making. American politicians, lured into unilateralism, may spurn international treaties and courts; but September 11 has been a warning that they do so at national peril. World wars in the 20th century were colossal versions of this warning. It turns out that national and international security are interdependent in the 21st—a statement of fact with heavy implication for ethical policymaking.

5. *It should advance the general welfare of all the inhabitants of the region in question and not become a tool by which powerful elites further cement their power.* As recent intervention experiences demonstrate, this is one of the most difficult principles to implement among all the seven. When governments and NGOs finally got around to helping at least the refugees who flooded into Congo camps, the Hutu *genocidaires* infiltrated the camps and came virtually to control them. As of 2001, the Bosnian elites who committed their own share of war crimes in 1992–95, still control enough government to siphon off chunks of international aid meant for rebuilding the countrywide economy. The political and ethical conflicts here are severe: if it is to avoid a new form of colonialism, intervention must be temporary. It must aim at establishing new leadership for protecting citizen lives without ignoring citizen democratic rights. For practical reasons it must often work with local elites who come to peace with records tarnished as perpetrators of injustice in war. Some of the compromises that the American government has made with local elites, *e.g.*, in Latin America, have precipitated the worldwide image of the U.S. as willing to support any "local elite" in the service of our own economic interest. If

---

rial interest can fortify the humanitarian. Such phenomena also fortify the theory that principles and consequences both belong in ethical reasoning, whether in personal or political settings.

our State Department and CIA had been as determined to save the lives of Indians in Guatemala as we are now claiming to save lives in Bosnia and Kosovo, accusations of hypocrisy in our support of "humanitarian intervention" would have less currency. Here, as in other recollections of national and international responsibility for good and evil, a day of commitment to quell genocide could be signaled and strengthened if political leaders would confess certain sins of the past they are determined not to repeat.

Justice is an elusive, approximate achievement in any society. Just peacemaking is no more an exact science than is just warmaking. As the Presbyterian document observes in one place, peacekeeping and peacemaking require "wise discernment and enormous patience," willingness to learn from mistakes, and awareness that "there are no quick fixes in peace anymore than there are costless wars." This truth poses great challenges to political leaders in a democracy, especially in the United States, whose citizens are not noted for their ideological tolerance of either policy-ambiguity or long costly wars.[9]

6. *Intervention should involve a minimum degree of coercion necessary to achieve the purposes of the action.* As stated, this principle duplicates one of the norms of the just war tradition, but it conflicts with the doctrine of "overwhelming force" favored by General Colin Powell in the Gulf War. Presumably the general favored the principle of discrimination with its support of "surgical strikes" at military installations of an enemy. Given the exigencies of warfare, military leaders are bound to distrust reliance on this norm; and the Gulf War alone left many Americans disturbed at the probable number of Iraqi soldiers killed by the overwhelming forces of the attacking allies. Who is to judge minima? In a democracy, presumably, political leadership ought to have the final say. What is the minimum necessary for success? For answering both questions civilian leaders are apt to depend upon the expertise of the military. In many ways this is one of the most troubling principles of the seven, for the history of wars is littered with excessive deaths deemed at the time to be necessary for "success." The city-bombings of World War II continue to haunt the memory of all of us who lived through that era. We remember that even

---

9 Research backs up the view of Professor Don M. Snider (Professor of Political Science at West Point) that the American public, if properly informed of the national interest and the likelihood of the venture's success, will tolerate military casualties. "Research has repeatedly demonstrated that there is room for political leaders to shape public opinion and create a forum for deliberation and debate of intervention decisions." Snider links this view with his account of the military vocation: "By gaining the right to kill . . . soldiers have given up the right not to be killed. Non-combatants have not gained the right to kill, and, as such, still retain their right not to be killed." By a large majority, says Snider, Americans understand this. *Cf.* DON M. SNIDER, JOHN A. NAGL, & TONY PFAFF, ARMY PROFESSIONALISM, THE MILITARY ETHIC, AND OFFICERSHIP IN THE 21ST CENTURY, 24, 31 (1999).

the atomic bombing of Hiroshima was justified at the time by the claim that it was the minimum necessary.

7. *Intervention in the form of punitive sanctions should be targeted against those in authority rather than against broad population groups.* Agreement with this principle lies behind a growing Western consensus that sanctions still in force against Iraq are immoral. Suppose that those in authority are willing for any number of children, women, and old people to suffer disease and starvation as the cost of maintaining the current government. Sanctions against South Africa in the 1980s were often criticized as mostly harming workers, not the capitalist classes. But sanctions brought pressures upon that government to change and thus, with other forces, helped deflect a looming civil war. Ten years of sanctions against Iraq have apparently not contributed much to the same goal there. Dictatorships are not easily overthrown by an increase in the suffering of their citizens. The case of Nazi Germany offered a grim instance of that.

As this is written, we do not know how successful the American military effort in Afghanistan will be judged in light of this principle. Formally the "war" against terrorism targets terrorists, but at what cost to non-terrorists? The just war doctrine of proportionality, along with discrimination, rises up to critique every slide into "total war," which is a synonym for war divorced utterly from ethics.

A CONTEXTUAL CONCLUSION

The 1998 Presbyterian statement concludes with an array of cautions about the imperfections of all human politics and all use of violence in those politics. Military intervention, no matter how humanely intended, will come to grief if it is not preceded, accompanied, and followed by other peace building measures quite different from military threat. A human rights regimen, courts of law, economic development, elections, nongovernmental service organizations, police training, disarmament of guerillas, and truth commissions may all be necessary for the rehabilitation of a society torn apart by internal war or threat thereof. Contemporary Bosnia is a sobering lesson in the need of all these elements for the rebuilding of a civil society. As of 2001, most residents of the country testify that economic development and honest government are the chief long-range barriers to renewed war there; but, they also say, the presence of UN troops for the foreseeable future is equally necessary. " Were they to leave today, Bosnia would go back to war."[10]

Throughout the 29 pages of this Presbyterian document, its authors try to make clear to their church constituents that they have responsibilities, as citizens and as members of a religious organization, to lift up

---

[10] Cf. Donald W. Shriver, *Bosnia In Fear and Hope*, XVIII World Pol'y J., No. 2, 49 (Summer 2001).

these principles for government action and to embody them in church teaching and action. Only in a context of reliance on extra-military contributions to peace will the military element make moral or practical sense. Among the policy and program recommendations commended:

- Pressure by the church on the U.S. government to increase its budget for international economic aid, which currently has shrunk to a pitiful proportion of the federal budget—approximately one-tenth of one percent.
- Reduction of the world arms trade, to which the United States is the major contributor, and the abolition of nuclear weapons, which by their nature violate the principle of discrimination.
- Advocacy of human rights as enumerated in the United Nations Declaration of 1948, increased support of the UN by the United States, and U.S. approval of the International Criminal Court.
- Peacemaking initiatives on the part of NGOs, including churches, to resolve conflicts in ways not always open to governments, *e.g.*, work with local church leaders for conflict transformation such as has been undertaken with some success by Presbyterians in the Sudan.
- Vigorous promotion of education and discussion of these issues in local congregations, taking advantage of the fact that churches have as much freedom for exploring these matters locally as does any other American institution.

The concluding paragraphs of this "Just Peacemaking" document strike a sobering note. In the spirit of both medieval Catholic and 16th century Calvinist thought, the document as a whole has sought to avoid the ethical extremes of both pacifism and the crusade. Like the older just war theory, the just peacemaking theory here shies away from frequent use of references to God and from simplistic definitions of political right and wrong. Throughout, the authors have tried to address new world conditions that prompt rethinking of old ethical stances. They are sure that both war and peace, in the 21st century, require new human grappling with the intersections of aspiration and circumstance.

> Unlike just war teaching, which has too often tended to focus too narrowly on the specific moral issues of using violent means to achieve political aims, just peace thinking must be taken as a holistic concern. Hence, it involves a shifting from a reactive stance (which considers whether or not a particular kind of action is legitimate once it has arisen) to a proactive stance (which thinks ahead as to what can be done to prevent the rise of a moral problem).

Secular critics of this church effort to think ethically about war and peace, along with many sectarian Christian traditionalists, incline towards dismissal of all theologizing about human political affairs as either irrelevant or presumptuous. History will test the relevance of such church-based effort, but this particular one should not be accused of Protestant *chutzpah.* Its rhetoric is sober, cautious, and exploratory.

> [W]e must recognize that it is difficult to discern all the consequences of massive political and military ventures. This makes careful discernment imperative, and willingness to revise politics in light of experience necessary. While resolve is crucial, as it is in all moral action, so is humility. Caution about the use of military force is always in order, yet the impulse of much political life is to stress the need for resolute action and determined resolve in ways that go against the very moral questioning that is crucial to the prophetic [religious] function. . . . Traditional just war teaching makes a point of entering conflict with the right intentions. That has generally been understood to rule out vindictiveness or self-aggrandizement. The pursuit of just peace enlarges the concerns beyond just war teaching. Not only must vindictiveness be avoided; wise discernment and enormous patience will be called for.[11]

Present in this language are words that, in September 2001, an American president has uttered in his call to his nation to respond militarily to terrorist attacks on two of our cities: resolve, patience, justice. Absent from the Presbyterian language are words which this president has also used: "infinite justice," "crusade," and "ridding the world of evil." Some of us must detect irony in the resistance of theologians to absolutist language and the temptation of politicians to resort to it. These American theologians, at least, are partial to the bedrock assumption of their discipline that was cogently expressed by one of their predecessors: "We all have a right to views of the Absolute, but none of us has a right to absolute views."[12] Which makes humility, in church and state, a first and last ethical word.

---

11 Resolution passed by the General Assembly of the Presbyterian Church of the United States in 1999.

12 Quoted from a lecture by H. Reinhold Niebuhr, winter semester 1956, Yale University Divinity School.

SECTION 2

THE LAW OF NATIONS

Even if the religious leaders of the three Abrahamic faith traditions were agreed on the role of force they could not prescribe what combatants may or may not do, as they could in earlier times: religion no longer has control over the use of force. Ultimately that authority resides with the hundred-odd states, which are still key actors in "the new international order" and both the beneficiaries and the users of international law.

That law is viewed by many as weak, ambiguous and ineffective, especially since its enforcement depends on agreement among the states that are theoretically bound by it. Nevertheless, it does provide guidelines for behavior and a basis for reaching judgments about the legality—and consequently the morality—of actions by states, by warring groups and by individuals. What do these guidelines have to say about the circumstances under which force may be utilized? About the ways in which it may be employed, *i.e.*, what constraints are placed on the types of weapons that may be used and the targets against which they may be directed? When religion has influenced the shaping of international law, how has it done so? Could it have greater influence, and if so would this lead to a better end?

As Professor James T. Johnson notes at the beginning of his chapter, positive international law in the 20th century sought to prevent interstate conflicts by disallowing the first resort to force; it has approved the use of force by states for only one reason, defense; and it has allowed the internationally sanctioned use of force only to preserve the peace and security of the international order, and then only at the decision of the Security Council and under its auspices.[1] One problem is that these constraints have sometimes been shrugged aside as states pursue what they consider their paramount interests, whether these be the ouster of unpalatable foreign leaders or the seizure of strategically important or economically valuable territory. Another, and perhaps more important, problem is that these constraints may impede actions designed to prevent or halt grave violations of human rights by or within a state, which can cite

1 *See infra* Ch. 4.

"sovereignty" as a barrier to external intervention. And while the international community is moving toward establishing criteria which must be met if sovereignty is to be respected, it has neither arrived at an agreed definition nor specified permissible ways in which these criteria can be enforced. Thus one of our questions, both raised and discussed by Professor Johnson, is whether one should, and if so how one can, redefine the circumstances under which force may lawfully be utilized to establish a "just peace."

As for the ways in which force may be employed, there are literally dozens of understandings, agreements and treaties prohibiting everything from the use of dum-dum bullets to the targeting of noncombatants as a means of making war. Sometimes, as in the Rwandan genocide, and terrorist bombings in Ireland and in Sri Lanka, actions against civilians are taken by nonstate actors; sometimes, as in ethnic cleansing in Yugoslavia and Sudan, by governments, sometimes, as in Israel/Palestine by both, but whatever their sponsorship they are generally regarded as immoral and condemned in principle, if not always in practice.[2] More problematic, because they are of a different nature, are attacks by armed forces on military targets which cause what some may regard as excessive "collateral damage." Here the problems are manifold, ranging from technical difficulties (even "smart bombs" sometimes behave stupidly) through clashes between the principles of law and the operational requirements of the military to the views of political leaders about the primacy of political objectives over ethical norms. This indeed is a problem which interfaces with religious principles on the one hand and the conduct of foreign policy on the other, as the next section indicates.

Before turning to it, there are two aspects of the formulation and implementation of international law which should be mentioned. The first is that that law by and large incorporates *Christian* principles and approaches, beginning with their introduction by Hugo Grotius in 1625; moreover, as Professor Johnson notes, both Grotius and other political philosophers built on the "just war" theory derived from Christian canon law.[3] Although the developments and refinements of international law in the 20th century stemmed from a variety of sources (lawyers, military officers, public officials, etc.) of all conceivable ethnic groups and religious persuasions, there was no systemic religious input comparable to that of Christianity; indeed, Islamic law emphasized faith-based interactions rather than those among states and hence could not be fitted into the framework of the League of Nations and the United Nations. And while this may not be of practical importance, it may fuel the sentiment expressed by some Muslims that the UN is a "foreign" entity.

---

2 As one Palestinian leader reportedly said with respect to terrorist attacks, "If we had the same weapons as the Israelis, we could fight them in ways acceptable to the Americans." N.Y. TIMES.

3 *See infra* Ch. 4.

The second matter of concern is the inequality in the power of member states: the only thing the Cocos Islands, with 6,000 inhabitants, has in common with China is that their names both begin with "C." This means to paraphrase one of George Orwell's phrases from *Animal Farm*, that "While all members are equal, some are more equal than others," both in the formulation of laws regarding the use of force and in their implementation. Thus, compellence is never practiced by the weak against the strong nor can the former effectively coerce the latter—save perhaps through terrorism. While this situation is no different from that prevailing in earlier years, it does, in this new age, affect both the ability to reach consensus about the uses of force and the ability to act on that consensus, once reached.

CHAPTER 4

THE LAW OF NATIONS: RELIGION, ETHICS AND INTERNATIONAL LAW BEARING ON CONFLICT AND PEACE

*Dr. James Turner Johnson**

THE PROBLEMATIC NATURE OF CONTEMPORARY ARMED CONFLICT

Contemporary armed conflict poses numerous problems for the conception and application of international law, for religious reflection on conflict and peace, and for identifying and drawing out the implications of moral values and maintaining ethical standards of conduct. Such conflict has more often than not been internal to states; yet the most settled international law on the use of force and the maintenance of peace has to do with regulating relations between and among states, and there remains a vigorous debate over the rights of states to intervene in internal conflicts and, conversely, their rights not to be the object of intervention in such cases. As for religious reflection, the shape of contemporary armed conflicts has occasioned a significant shift away from the antiwar, antimilitary rhetoric so widespread during the Cold War to frequent advocacy of military intervention to protect aid workers and/or facilitate delivery of aid, to guard religiously or ethnically defined populations from human rights abuse, and to help toward reconciliation of societies torn by internal conflict. The result has been a new map of positions on conflict and peace, reshuffling the relationships between former allies and adversaries in ways that are not yet entirely sorted out. At the same time, the religious debate has had to come to terms with the fact that religious belief has at times been employed to foment conflict and inflame it, while religious identity has in some conflicts been used as a marker of friends and foes; this complicates the effort of many in the religious debate over conflict and peace to represent religion as offering resources for reconciliation and peace in war-torn societies. As for the

* Rutgers University.

sphere of ethics, contemporary armed conflict has forced rethinking of the degree to which values, such as human rights, and limits on violence, such as avoidance of harm to noncombatants, are indeed universal, and what is necessary to maintain them.

These challenges posed by contemporary armed conflict affect international law, religion, and ethics both separately and together. In this chapter I will focus on the area of overlap of these challenges and the possibilities for commonality in meeting them, but this will also require notice of some of the most distinctive problems for each field. I will first look at the shape of contemporary international law on armed conflict and peace, then discuss some important interrelations among international law, religion, and ethics on approaches to conflict and peace, and finally identify four particular problems affecting all three fields, whose resolution requires sustained use of the resources of all three.

THE SHAPE OF CONTEMPORARY INTERNATIONAL LAW ON ARMED CONFLICT AND PEACE

This section begins with a survey of the relevant positive law on the resort to armed force, the restraints governing use of such force, and the state of peace, then briefly examines some of the disagreements over how to apply this law in contemporary circumstances and over the relationship between the positive law and customary law.

On the resort to armed force, positive international law, as established in the United Nations Charter, restricted lawful resort to arms to response to two conditions: individual or collective self-defense against armed attack and action under the auspices of the United Nations Security Council to remedy a threat to international peace and security, as determined by the Security Council. The relevant positive law provisions are Article 2 (4) against the threat or use of armed force in interstate disputes, Article 51 on the right to use such force for individual or collective self-defense, and Chapter 7 generally on the right to use armed force under Security Council auspices against threats to international peace and security. Behind the Charter provisions lay the earlier effort in the League of Nations Covenant to reduce recourse to war by interposing appeals to arbitration and the agreement of the signatories of the Kellogg-Briand Pact (Pact of Paris, 1928) not to take first resort to force in disputes with other signatories. That is, the development of 20th-century positive international law focused on uses of armed force between or among states; it sought to prevent interstate conflicts by disallowing the first resort to force; it permitted the use of force by states for only one reason, defense; and it allowed internationally sanctioned resort to force only to preserve the peace and security of the international order, and then only at the decision of the Security Council and under its auspices. This may seem straightforward and simple, and indeed it does to some. Yet every single one of these provisions is challenged in the debate over contemporary armed conflict, as I will illustrate a bit later.

The positive law on the restraints to be observed in the use of armed force is defined by the law of armed conflicts. This portion of international law has historically had two main foci: the definition of certain classes of people and property as deserving of protection during armed conflict and the definition of such protection in each case, and the limitation of weapons deemed to be indiscriminate or to cause unnecessary destruction or suffering. In its present form it addresses not only formally declared wars between or among states but also other forms of armed conflict, whether international or noninternational.[1] The introduction of the idea of "crimes against humanity" (not explicitly specified in the codified international agreements) in the Nuremberg and Tokyo trials, the definition and outlawing of genocide in 1948, and the development of international human rights law over the last half century have added to these traditional concerns of the law of armed conflicts, and some contemporary commentators accordingly treat them under one rubric: international humanitarian law. Others, including military lawyers, deal with the law of armed conflicts and human rights law as separate though interrelated. The charges to the current international tribunals for Rwanda and the former Yugoslavia give them jurisdiction over violations of all these sorts of provisions of international positive law.

Positive international law has traditionally handled peace, like war, as a matter of relations between and among states. This mirrors the historical customary law, in which peace was sometimes effectively treated as the condition of not being at war and at other times, as in the "perpetual peace" movement of the 18th and 19th centuries, treated as a state of mutual security to be achieved through the establishment of international order. Both these conceptions of peace are found in the Charter of the United Nations, with its emphasis on avoidance of conflict, common agreement on standards of conduct and interactions, and provision for policing threats or breaches of the peace. A central concept in both the traditional and contemporary understandings of peace is the idea of sovereignty as originally defined in the Treaty of Westphalia and provisions for the protection of such sovereignty.

The idea of peace thus understood in relation to interstate relations has proven somewhat difficult to extend into intrastate conflicts. There are two major problems, the first having to do with the need for sovereign authority to maintain peace, the second having to do with the need

---

1 For compilations of specific elements of this law, *see.* THE LAW OF WAR: A DOCUMENTARY HISTORY (Leon Friedman ed., 1972); DOCUMENTS ON THE LAWS OF WAR (Adam Robers & Richard Guelff ed., 2d ed. 1989).

for a fabric of domestic institutions and relations within which peaceful interaction can take place.

First, peace between and among states requires the action of a functioning authority in each state able to exercise sovereign power in a recognizable way; in intrastate conflicts, this authority may be lacking on one side or both, or, if present, it may act in such as way as to undercut its right to be treated as sovereign. These difficulties are amply illustrated by recent intrastate armed conflicts. Putting the matter more sharply, a major difficulty in extending the international law idea of peace to intrastate conflicts has to do with the adequacy of the Westphalian conception of sovereignty when applied to a failed state or to a state whose government uses its power for gross violations of human rights or even genocide. I will return to this problem of sovereignty in the last part of this Chapter.

The second major problem posed for the international law idea of peace in the context of contemporary intrastate armed conflicts is that the nature of such conflicts destroys the internal institutions and patterns of relationships necessary for a peacefully functioning society. Just as the United Nations itself was aimed at establishing a frame for peacefully functioning interrelationships between nations after World War II, so means have to be found to restore patterns of interrelationship in everyday life that allow for peaceful interaction after an armed conflict internal to a society has been successfully brought to an end. Unfortunately, there is no clear one-size-fits-all blueprint for doing this, and there have been chronic lapses of will and of resources besides. Again, I will return to this problem of reconstructing peace after an internal armed conflict in the last part of this chapter.

A complicating factor is that there are significant differences of judgment as to how to understand and apply the provisions of positive international law in particular contemporary situations, as well as differences over the weight to be given to the positive law and to other factors. In particular much debate has been directed to the question of military intervention in intrastate armed conflicts. UN Secretary-General Kofi Annan has argued in various contexts that such intervention is justified according to the Charter provided it is for humanitarian purposes, a position supported by positive law provisions regarding war crimes, human rights, and genocide. Against this is the traditional understanding of state sovereignty; so the issue is the degree to which this understanding has been eroded by the development of positive international law. Clearly, the Security Council may authorize intervention in cases when a conflict is determined to be a threat to international peace and security, but not everyone agrees that such a finding is necessary in every case. One example of an argument that engages such issues is that of South African Justice Richard Goldstone, former chief prosecutor for the International Criminal

Tribunals for Rwanda and the former Yugoslavia, on the case of Kosovo. He begins by observing, "There can be no question that the military intervention in Kosovo by NATO constituted a breach of the United Nations Charter," specifically Article 2(4). Yet, he continues, "[t]here are serious and important reasons for questioning the appropriateness and the applicability of that Charter provision at the beginning of the twenty-first century." He cites three: the "erosion of national sovereignty with the internationalization of human rights," the increasing porousness of national boundaries, "especially in consequence of human rights violations," and third, the "vastly changed political map and distribution of power" today as compared to 1945.[2] Thus, Goldstone's argument is that developments in international law and the shape of the international order since the adoption of the Charter have modified the seemingly clear prohibition of interventionary use of force found there. In particular, for him the growth of international human rights law has seriously modified the rights and protections of sovereignty, with the implication that the anti-force rules in the Charter do not mean what they once did. That is, the law has changed, and the circumstances for applying the law have also changed. Goldstone's argument recalls but goes beyond Julius Stone's 1958 reasoning that the Charter's prohibition of force "seems conditioned on the assumption that effective collective measures can be taken under the Charter to bring about adjustment or settlement 'in conformity with the principles of justice and international law,'" and that it is not clear what the law requires when such measures have failed or never existed.[3] The Foreign Affairs Committee of the British House of Commons put the matter squarely as one of conflict between law and morality, writing: "[W]e conclude that NATO's military action, if of dubious legality in the current state of international law, was justified on moral grounds."[4] A still different line of argument follows from the realization that, in the customary law, regional hegemons have been allowed considerable latitude in intervening by force to discipline states within their spheres of interest, so that whatever one argues about the requirements of the positive law, NATO was acting within the range of the customary law.

My own position, which I have developed in detail elsewhere,[5] is that in cases of egregious violations of human rights or breakdowns in the provision of fundamental human needs as a result of an armed conflict, groups of states (whether formal alliances or *ad hoc* coalitions) or

---

2 RICHARD J. GOLDSTONE, KOSOVO: AN ASSESSMENT IN THE CONTEXT OF INTERNATIONAL LAW 16 (2000).

3 JULIUS STONE, AGGRESSION AND WORLD ORDER (1958).

4 HOUSE OF COMMONS, SELECT COMMITTEE ON FOREIGN AFFAIRS, FOURTH REPORT (2000), available at http://www.publications.parliament.uk/pa/cm199900/cmselect/cmfaff/28/2813/htm.

5 JAMES TURNER JOHNSON, MORALITY AND CONTEMPORARY WARFARE Ch. 3 (1999).

even individual states may intervene militarily to remedy the need. While Security Council authorization may be sought, it is not required as matters now stand.

In the context of this chapter, I offer these observations on the debate over intervention simply to illustrate the complexity involved in understanding how international law bears on the question of contemporary armed conflict and the quest for peace. I turn now to the question of how religion and ethics relate to this question. I will look at three issues: first, the historical and thematic connections between international law and the just war tradition of Western culture; second, the involvement of religion in the human rights debate; and third, three distinctive conceptions of the ideal of peace in Western religious and ethical thought.

INTERNATIONAL LAW, RELIGION, AND ETHICS: SEEING IMPORTANT CONNECTIONS

Since the work of James Brown Scott in the 1930s and the Carnegie Institute's series *Classics of International Law* published between the two World Wars it has been impossible to deny the historical and thematic links between the just war tradition and international law, especially the law of armed conflict. For Scott the focus of this linkage was particularly in the work of the Spanish theorist Francisco de Vitoria and his colleagues at the University of Salamanca.[6] Fundamentally he argued that through them the religiously shaped just war theory became a theory of international law based in natural law and *jus gentium*, leading ultimately to the coalescence of positive international law. In my own historical work on just war tradition and its relation to international law I have argued that other early modern theorists of just war and the law of war need also to be understood as helping to shape this transmission, and in my judgment there are two key figures, not one: Vitoria at the transition of medieval just war theory into conceptions and contexts of the modern era, and Grotius at the critical point of translation from the theoretical language of just war into the somewhat different theoretical language of modern international law.[7] But these differences over the actual nature of the transmission do not undermine our fundamental agreement about the historical and thematic connections between just war tradition and international law. I would argue that, moreover, the relationship continues. Medieval just war tradition was a consensus that included religious, legal, moral, and military components. In the modern era, as with other major elements of life and thought, these components have developed separately, producing distinctive traditions of thought and practice on war

---

6 JAMES BROWN SCOTT, THE SPANISH ORIGIN OF INTERNATIONAL LAW (1934).

7 JAMES TURNER JOHNSON, IDEOLOGY, REASON, AND THE LIMITATION OF WAR 150–258 (1975); JAMES TURNER JOHNSON, JUST WAR TRADITION AND THE RESTRAIN OF WAR 172–89 (1981).

and peace in religion, law, ethics, and military life. Yet these are still historically and thematically related, and fruitful conversation among them is not only possible because of this, but also important for all of them as providing a fuller perspective on a common subject.[8]

There are fundamental structural and thematic parallels between just war tradition in its classic form and the provisions of positive international law relating to use of armed force. There are also important differences, which are in part the reflection of the different character of moral reflection and law and in part the result of historical influences.[9] If the parallels make conversation possible, the differences make it necessary. On the matter of resort to use of armed force, there seems at first look to be a substantive difference in the idea of just cause between international law's focus on defense and just war tradition's allowance also for retaking that which has been wrongly taken and punishment of evil. But on closer look, one quickly discovers that the concept of defense in international law also allows retaliation, which is one form of punishment of evil, and retaking what has been wrongly taken, by defining it as defense against armed attack still in progress as long as the attacker wrongly holds territory, property, or persons wrongly seized. So there is a great deal more in common to talk about here than first meets the eye. Similarly, on the matter of the authority necessary for resort to armed force, both international law and just war tradition define this tradition in terms of sovereignty; yet the contents of the idea of sovereignty in each case are somewhat different. The important questions have to do with the extent of state sovereignty regarding the use of force and the degree to which the United Nations may be said to be actually possessed of sovereign authority to use force. One might continue on through the full list of relevant criteria for resort to force and for restraint in the use of force, but my point here is only to illustrate the relationship that makes conversation between these two traditions possible, suggests that it is necessary, and holds out the promise that it might be fruitful. At the end of this chapter, as already mentioned, I will return to several of the questions raised in common here and pursue them further for the context of contemporary armed conflict.

Of course, to point to the historical connections, agreements, and differences between just war tradition and international law is not specifically to speak of the relation of religious teaching to international law. The chapters by Shriver, Gopin, and Sachedina in this volume exemplify approaches each of which, on their own terms, would have to be brought

---

8 *See further* James Turner Johnson, Just War Tradition and the Restraint of War 190–366 (1981).

9 On these parallels and differences, *see further* James Turner Johnson, Morality and Contemporary Warfare 28–30 (1999).

into dialogue with the provisions of international law. Still, a bit more can be said. Christian thinking helped importantly to shape the idea of just war as it came together in the Middle Ages, and in the modern period, specifically, Christian versions of just war reasoning have formed a major stream of the developing tradition. While there was no explicitly Jewish input into the early formation of just war reasoning, elements from the Old Testament played central roles there, and over the past 50 years Jewish thinkers have developed what has sometimes been called a "Jewish just war doctrine," closely paralleling the concerns of just war tradition, based on interpretations of halakhic ideas and precedents. Gopin's chapter highlights some of this development. As for Islam, its own tradition on *siyar* (international relations), including normative conceptions of peace and war, began to take shape as early as the eighth century. The principal question here is how this can be brought into dialogue with international law and with the underlying broad tradition of just war. On the level of state relations, the fact of membership in the United Nations and agreement to the provisions of international law argues that predominantly Muslim states, like others, have accepted the obligations laid down in international law. Only for Islamic radicals is this problematic, for they hold that Islamic law inherently supersedes international law. The logic of this position is rejection of international law and separation from international institutions and agreements. But a significant body of reasoning argues that international law either derives historically from Islamic law (via the influence Islamic religion and culture had on medieval Europe) or, so far as it reflects the divinely created order of the world, presumptively does not diverge from Islamic law. These approaches open the door to dialogue over the shape and meaning of international law, dialogue much like that possible from a just war perspective.

Let me now turn to the second theme of this part of the chapter, religion and the debate over human rights. One of the features common to moral thought, political theory, and law during the modern period has been a shift away from the language of natural law, first to that of natural rights in Hobbes, Locke, and the French *Philosophes*, and then to that of human rights, especially in the period since the Universal Declaration of Human Rights in 1948. While the use of the idea and language of rights in the political and legal fields is older than that in religious discourse, a substantial and still growing body of literature connects Western ideas of rights to the religious conceptions of Judaism and Christianity. Alongside this, another body of literature is also developing that connects fundamental ideas of rights to themes and concepts in other major world religions. The Project on Religion and Human Rights has, for example, argued that there are historical, social, and scriptural links between core human rights ideas and the major religions of the world, linking conceptions of human dignity to the identification of such rights and the obligation to respect them.[10] At the same time, the underlying idea that the idea of human rights is universal, welling up in religious consciousness the world over, is in tension with the diversity that is encountered when the various religions and their associated cultures are examined on their own terms.[11] Such tension is also, of course, to be found in the body of international statements, agreements, and other documents defining various kinds of rights to be recognized and respected within the frame of world order.

Where the subject is armed conflict, the matter is somewhat clearer. On the one hand, the law of armed conflict lays out specific requirements of protection and avoidance of direct, intentional harm, and though it does not base these provisions explicitly on the idea of rights, the provisions themselves establish certain rights. At first limited to international wars only, these provisions and the associated rights have applied, since the 1949 Geneva Conventions, to armed conflicts even if they are not formal wars and regardless of whether they are internal or between states. The Genocide Convention similarly has established certain rights and the protections owed them. At the same time, religious discourse on respect for and protection of human rights in relation to armed conflict has focused on the need to respond to violations of the most flagrant and extreme sort of those rights taken to be the most fundamental. In this way religious discourse has sought to focus the issue by concentrating on what is most widely agreed upon. Let me illustrate this by specific reference to an example of recent religious thought on human rights in connection with armed conflict and peace, the United States Catholic Conference's 1993 statement, *The Harvest of Justice Is Sown in Peace* (National Conference of Catholic Bishops 1993; hereafter NCCB 1993). In a section titled "Securing Human Rights" the statement speaks of these rights as including "the full spectrum of civil, political, social, cultural, and economic rights" and observes that "[p]romotion of the full complement of human rights and religious liberty has been and remains a central priority of our conference."[12] This "full spectrum" is, of course, precisely what is differently defined in each major religious tradition of the world. Thus a few pages later, when the immediate subject is humanitarian intervention, the focus has shifted to egregious violations of basic rights. Pope John Paul II is quoted to this effect, "urging that 'humanitarian intervention be obligatory where the survival of populations and entire ethnic groups is seriously compromised'."[13] In their own language, the bishops argue that "the principles of sovereignty and nonintervention [in international law] may be overridden by forceful means in exceptional circumstances, notably

---

10 Religion and Human Rights 63–71 (John Kelsay & Sumner B. Twiss eds., 1994).

11 *Cf. id.* at 31–59.

12 NCCB 1993:9.

13 *Id.* at 15.

in the cases of genocide or when whole populations are threatened by aggression or anarchy," and that military intervention may be justified "to ensure that starving children can be fed or that whole populations will not be slaughtered."[14] This thinking, in short, leads to three general conclusions: first, that despite diversity in the identification of the full spectrum of human rights and the kind of protection they should enjoy, everyone should be able to agree on certain basic human rights and agree that they should not be grossly violated; second, that such violation of these basic rights establishes not only a just cause but also a moral obligation to use force to end the violations and reestablish the protections, and third, that the nature of the armed intervention must not itself violate these basic rights. From one perspective this is an extremely minimal set of propositions, but from another it is quite aggressive in its implications for thinking about moral responsibility toward contemporary conflicts.

The idea of peace focuses the relations among religion, ethics, and international law in its own ways. Western religion has developed three distinct ways of thinking about the ideal of peace in human society and how to achieve it. One is, of course, just war tradition, in which the goal of establishing peace is one of the necessary conditions for resort to armed force in face of injustice. This requirement of peace also bears on right conduct in use of force, for thematically how one fights cannot be separated from why one is fighting. The second broad way of thinking religiously about peace is that rooted in the tradition of sectarian rejection of the world and efforts to withdraw from it so as to eliminate its evils, including violence. In the modern version of this tradition, as found in the teaching of the so-called "historic peace churches," the focus is on the moral and political rejection of violence, understood as inherently evil; peace is the result of this rejection. The third religiously based way of thinking about peace and its achievement aims at establishing a structure of world order in which war would be abolished. In specifically religious discourse this conception of how to achieve peace is closely related to the idea of the Kingdom of God on earth as the goal of history.[15]

Considered separately, these three traditions of Western religious thought define the world and its possibilities differently and thus think of the place of force differently. For the historical sectarian position the world is inherently and unreformably evil; it is marked by sin from its depths to its heights, and its justice is injustice, its order disorder. Its use of force is accordingly evil, since by definition it can serve no good. The contemporary peace churches modify this to identify all violence, what-

---

[14] *Id.* at 16.

[15] I treat these three approaches to peace in detail in JAMES TURNER JOHNSON, THE QUEST FOR PEACE: THREE MORAL TRADITIONS IN WESTERN CULTURAL HISTORY (1987).

ever its reasons, as evil. Peace and a just social order can be possible only through the moral and political rejection of violence. For the world order tradition the world is capable of being transformed into a just order; the problem is to find the right structure and get general assent to it. Violence will in the end disappear, but in the period when the world order is still forming, it may have recourse to force for the purpose of the end result; thus all uses of force for other reasons are bad, as by definition they cannot serve the order, justice, and peace of the higher community. Just war tradition falls in between: the world includes evil, but it also has potential for some good. Its order and justice are not perfect, but they are better than disorder (or evil order) and injustice. Similarly, its peace is imperfect, but the peace of just order is better than the stability imposed by unjust tyranny. Thus force may be used for order and justice, to the end of peace. These are importantly different understandings of peace, its relation to human politics, and the place of the use of force in relation to its achievement.

CONTEMPORARY DIALOGUE BETWEEN RELIGION AND LAW OVER THE PROBLEM OF ARMED CONFLICT

The three traditional approaches to the idea of peace are all to be found in contemporary dialogue between religion and law over the problem of armed conflict, though there is a significant area of overlap between the contemporary heirs of the world-rejection and the world-order approaches. The pacifism of rejection of the world is found, of course, in those religious groups which maintain, to a greater or lesser degree, the emphasis of the Radical Reformation on creating and living in Christian communities apart from involvement in worldly life. At the extreme of this position there is no dialogue with the world as a matter of principle. Closer to the mainstream of American religious life, though, stand theologians like the late Mennonite thinker John Howard Yoder and Methodist Stanley Hauweras (strongly influenced by Yoder), who reject violence as opposed to the ethic of Jesus and argue that the church must conform to this ethic while seeking to offer alternatives to violence in the world. I discuss Hauerwas' position below as representing the first traditional type of approach to conflict and peace in the contemporary debate. Broadly representing the world-order tradition is the approach widely called "positive peacemaking," which seeks to head off potential conflicts and to deal with existing conflicts by a range of measures, from work by individuals and religiously sponsored organizations to diplomatic efforts, that do not involve use of armed force. I treat this position below by examining a recent collection of essays."[16] The third approach, building out of

16 JUST PEACEMAKING: TEN PRACTICES FOR ABOLISHING WAR (Glen Stassen ed., 1998).

just war tradition, envisions the use of such force as a possible agency toward the ending of conflict and the creation of a just and peaceful social order in the aftermath of conflict. In the following discussion I treat this approach by examining the position of the United States Catholic bishops in their 1993 statement, *The Harvest of Justice is Sown in Peace*, introduced earlier in connection with the discussion of human rights. The line between the first two approaches is blurred by the fact that the "positive peacekeeping" approach is supported by many from the peace-church background who are themselves absolute pacifists but rather than withdrawing from the world, seek to reform its institutions along the lines of the London Friends' statement quoted above. Similarly, the latter two approaches may agree on certain points with regard to how to deal with a particular conflict—for example, the importance of diplomatic initiatives and economic sanctions as an alternative to resort to armed force—though at their extremes they are clearly different, reflecting, respectively, the pacifist rejection of violent means and the just war acceptance of such means within the framework of the conditions defined by the *jus ad bellum* and the *jus in bello.*

Hauerwas' position, as already indicated, rejects violence entirely as incompatible with the ethic and model of Jesus. Individual Christians and the church as a whole are obliged to follow this model and act according to this ethic. Hauerwas describes this, for the church, as an obligation to act independently, in ways determined by its own choosing, without depending on the state or the state system. The church, thus understood, is an alternative to the state. Hauerwas insists that this way of thinking is not sectarian but simply the assertion that the church has its own agenda: is "a community schooled with skills provided by a truthful account of the world,"[17] namely, that of Christ's death and resurrection. He writes, "[W]e need to have our imaginations freed to consider alternatives to the nation-state. We must act, as Yoder describes the early Quakers doing in Pennsylvania, to create processes that make questions of violence irrelevant."[18] This may include urging the United States government "to take what is judged to be the least destructive stand" in its relations with other societies, but always the church should seek to create "conversation" as the means of resolving conflicts internal to or between states.[19] This position is clearly congruent with many of the activities of the peace churches, which today constitute themselves as a pacifist present and witness within the framework of the American state, and which operate an active ministry in societies torn by conflict, in which

---

17 Stanley Hauerwas, *Epilogue: A Pacifist response to the Bishops, in* Paul Ramsey Speak Up for Just War or Pacifism 149–82 (1988).

18 *Id.* at 180.

19 *Id.* at 182.

one of the main themes is reconciliation through interaction or, in Hauerwas' term, through creating "conversation."

These activities of the peace churches might also, from a different perspective, be included under the rubric of "positive peacemaking," an idea that takes many forms. Glen Stassen's *Just Peacemaking*[20] exemplifies the considerable variety of approaches that may be included under this rubric as well as an effort to mold them into a unified front. This book is important not so much in itself but as providing an encyclopedic view of the contemporary idea of "positive peacemaking." The variety found here is indicated by the diversity of the 22 contributors from various Christian denominations and the division of the book according to different "practices," which are in fact various approaches to defusing conflict. The effort to achieve a unified front is found in Stassen's argument that the book defines a "new ethic" of "just peacemaking" that is neither pacifism nor a form of just war thinking but an alternative to both. Stassen describes this "new ethic" as grounded in three theological principles: first, "a biblically informed concept of discipleship and peacemaking initiatives grounded in the life, teachings, death, and resurrection of Jesus Christ"; second, "a church committed to seek the peace of the city where its people dwell . . . by engaging the issues of peace and justice—especially justice—actively within the brokenness of the world"; third, "the church community as the eschatological presence of God's love and reign in the world, . . . [which seeks] to discern what just peacemaking means and to model peacemaking practices in our . . . lives."[21] Stassen and his colleagues argue that the ten particular "practices" by which the essays in the book are organized (further grouped into "peacemaking initiatives," "justice," and "love and community") follow from these theological principles.

Now, in truth the theological principles as stated are so broad as to be almost generic for American Christianity. Similarly, the differences between a Catholic political scientist and international relations specialist like Bruce Russett, one of the contributors, and Stassen himself, a Protestant absolute pacifist, are so considerable that one may wonder whether it is at all useful to think of them together as defining a distinctive "new ethic." Stassen claims that this "new ethic" is neither pacifism nor a form of just war thinking, but rather stands as an alternative to both. It would be more correct to say that, insofar as the ten practices are understood as ways of describing and creating new structures aimed at avoiding violent conflict or use of violence to respond to conflict, they map out a form of pacifism of the "world order" variety as discussed earlier. At the same time, if they are understood as examples of measures that

---

20 *Supra* note 16.

21 *Id* at 6.

might be taken short of resort to armed force, then they map very well the assumptions behind the just war requirement that use of force be a last resort.

My third example of current religious thought related to war and peace is the United States Catholic bishops' 1993 statement, *The Harvest of Justice.* The bishops' position differs from the others just discussed in that it explicitly undertakes to define just resort to force—armed intervention to respond to gross violations of basic human rights—as a moral option. But its frame is nonetheless that of "a strong presumption against the use of force," a presumption first embraced in the Catholic bishops' *The Challenge of Peace* a decade earlier.[22] The role of just war thinking here is to establish "the conditions when this presumption may be overridden."[23] The overriding emphasis is on "peacemaking," defined first in terms of the proper virtues for peacemakers (getting one's own heart right) and a vision of peace defined in terms of the primacy of the universal common good, the importance of social and economic development in creating conditions for a just and lasting peace, and "the moral imperative of solidarity between affluent, industrial nations and poor, developing ones."[24] This leads to a specific "agenda for peacemaking": strengthening global institutions, securing human rights, assuring sustainable and equitable development, restraining nationalism and eliminating religious violence, and building cooperative security. (Humanitarian intervention is the last of four topics treated under this last heading: the others are nuclear disarmament, demilitarization, and economic sanctions.)

All of these forms of contemporary religiously based thinking about war and peace define a tension in the relations between the religious community and the state, though there is a difference in degree among them as to whether the state is understood as part of the problem the religious community must overcome or part of the solution. A form of this tension is the distinction made by the Catholic bishops between the "affluent, industrial nations" and the "poor developing ones," where the religious community is represented as morally bound to side with the latter. Another form of tension with the state and the system of international law comes from the antipathy toward violence as such found in all three of the positions I have sketched; even the Catholic bishops' acceptance of use of armed force in some cases to overcome conflict is described as an exceptional case, overriding the general and more basic "presumption against the use of force."

---

22 NATIONAL CONFERENCE OF CATHOLIC BISHOPS, THE CHALLENGE OF PEACE: GOD'S PROMISE AND OUR RESPONSE (1983).

23 NCCB 1993:5.

24 *Id.* at 3.

All the forms of positive peacemaking here define violence as evil in itself and thus to be avoided. Hauerwas makes no bones about being an absolute pacifist, opposed to all violence; neither does Stassen, though some of his collaborators would accept limited uses of force under certain circumstances, as would the Catholic bishops despite their general "presumption" against it. One must thus ask a fundamental moral and religious question: is violence as such in fact always evil? If one says yes, then the interest-driven statecraft of political realism is rejected; so also is the law-driven statecraft of the United Nations and international law; so also is the justice-driven statecraft of the main line of just war tradition. As I have argued in other contexts, I think the Catholic bishops' idea of a general "presumption against the use of force" is outside the main thrust of this tradition.[25] Can accommodations be found? Hauerwas explicitly rejects the kind of compromise made by the U.S. Catholic bishops, effectively saying, let the church be the church (pacifist) and the state be the state (violent). For Stassen the resort to force is a move backwards toward a more primitive state of human development, whereas the ten practices he and his colleagues define are represented as progressive steps forward in the evolution of human societies. Even the Catholic bishops remain uneasy about the resort to force; while their support for humanitarian intervention by military means is strong, it is still treated as an exceptional response to outrageous and otherwise intractable conditions. At the time of Iraq's takeover of Kuwait, their spokesmen were among those urging that armed force not be used and that economic sanctions be tried and given more time to work instead.

My own preference is for a religion-based dialogue with law and statecraft over war and peace which follows the guidelines laid down in the main line of just war tradition as it has historically developed. The *a priori* rejection of all violence as inherently evil makes for bad statecraft. It is not necessary to reject violence as such to leave room for the practices described by the advocates of "positive peacemaking" within the frame of statecraft as defined by the international legal order and just war tradition, and even within the frame of the politics of interest. Indeed, it is difficult to see how, given the actual nature of the world, any quest for good politics—politics with the ends of a just and peaceful order—could proceed without the possibility of using armed force.

Once the determination has been made to use armed force in response to gross violations of human rights in an armed conflict, how should that force be used? If one begins by defining violence as itself evil, then the requirements of discrimination and proportionality must be narrowed ever more rigorously, and we have seen this in recent religiously

---

25 James Turner Johnson, Morality and Contemporary Warfare 35–36 (1999).

based criticism of interventionary uses of force. For example, the destruction of power grids, phone terminals, transportation corridors, and broadcasting facilities, which all have both civilian and military functions, is allowed in the law of armed conflict and is compatible with classic just war reasoning. Today, though, attacks on such "dual-use" targets are more likely to be challenged as a violation of proportionality, discrimination, or both, as in this observation by the U.S. Catholic bishops: "[T]he targeting of civilian infrastructure, which afflicts ordinary civilians long after war has ceased, can amount to making war on noncombatants."[26] If the infrastructure in question is in fact civilian (*i.e.*, noncombatant), then there should be no question that targeting it is making war on noncombatants; yet infrastructure typically has a dual-use function. In labeling the infrastructure civilian only, this sentence aims at putting it off limits for attack. Another way of narrowing the options allowed for moral use of armed force is to insist that discrimination requires not simply avoiding direct, intentional attacks on noncombatants but any attacks at all in which noncombatants will be harmed collaterally. Again, the U.S. Catholic bishops provide a convenient example of this position: "Strategies and tactics that lead to avoidable casualties are inconsistent with the underlying intention of the just war tradition."[27] The most extreme example of the use of the principles of discrimination and proportionality to narrow the possibility for moral uses of armed force has been around at least since the 1960s: the modern-war pacifist argument that all uses of armed force today are necessarily indiscriminate and disproportionate, so that there is no longer a possibility of a just war.

Now, I should say that I disagree with all these positions as stated. The position of modern-war pacifism both is factually incorrect and wrongly inverts the logic of just war reasoning. The treatment of proportionality and discrimination I have just sketched similarly misuses these criteria, as I understand their meaning in classic just war reasoning. If one begins with a presumption against war as the fundamental moral stance, then the dice are already loaded against use of armed force. To narrow the options for such use follows from this. To begin instead where I do, and where just war tradition has classically begun, is to understand the problem of peace in terms of creating a just order, not simply avoiding violence. Yet it is clear that much contemporary religious discourse about the use of armed force begins with a presumption that violence itself is always wrong and is to be ended. This leads to some significant tensions and real disagreements over the question of uses of military force in the contemporary world, including interventionary uses of force for protecting human rights.

---

26 NCCB 1993:6.

27 *Id.*

FOUR CONTEMPORARY ISSUES

I want to conclude this discussion by briefly treating four particular problems contemporary armed conflict poses for religious and ethical discourse and for international law. They have to do with the need for rethinking the idea of sovereignty, the use of the idea of human rights as a justification for use of armed force, the erosion of noncombatant immunity in contemporary armed conflict, and the practical meaning of the restoration of peace.

First, as to sovereignty, recent developments have exposed the limits of the Westphalian conception of sovereignty which has long been the norm for relations among states. This is the conception behind the UN Charter's prohibition of the use of force across national borders for the settlement of disputes, as well as its allowance of the use of force in self-defense against armed attack across a state's borders. This conception is at once territorial and formal: it attempts to hold stable the territorial borders of all states and it accepts as the government of a state whatever authority has been formally recognized by other states. Historically, it was an attempt to secure international stability by giving the status quo a normative status, and it has generally succeeded at this. By ruling out appeals to other kinds of normative claims to establish sovereign rights, it sought to avoid religiously motivated wars like the Thirty Years War. Whatever its past success at this, the rise of appeals not only to religion but to ideology and national or ethnic identity—appeals characteristic of contemporary armed conflict—suggest that the stability imposed by the Westphalian idea of sovereignty is under stress and perhaps breaking down. At the same time, appeals to the rights of sovereignty as defined territorially and formalistically have been used to shelter oppression, human rights violations, genocide, the development of weapons of mass destruction, and terrorism. There is, I suggest, a growing opinion that the idea of sovereignty must include a moral component, implying responsibilities as well as rights. The consensus on the idea of sovereignty before the Peace of Westphalia included such a moral component, but it was part of what was discarded in the definition of the new concept. One finds it clearly in medieval and early modern discussions of the good prince and the right exercise of sovereign rule. I would argue that a moral floor for the responsibilities of sovereignty is assumed in the establishment of international criminal tribunals able to try military and government authorities (up to the case of a head of state, as in the case of Slobodan Milosevic before the Tribunal for the Former Yugoslavia). The Taliban regime's violations of human rights in Afghanistan raise similar problems, which the support of international terrorism multiplies. Iraq's flaunting of United Nations arms inspection procedures (presumably so that its programs for developing weapons of mass destruction can continue) also exemplifies a case in which Iraq's head of state, Saddam Hussein, has violated the responsibilities of sovereignty is a matter on which there is less consensus. I would argue that this behavior too falls below the minimal requirements of morally responsible sovereignty. Whatever one thinks about these specific cases, my general point is that there needs to be a more focused, more sustained examination of what a moral element in the definition of sovereignty ought to be and what, if any, changes in international law and practice it might imply. Religious and moral discourse can contribute importantly to such an examination.

Second, the use of the idea of protecting human rights as a justifying cause for the use of armed force has brought into focus the discrepancies in existing international law and among cultures over exactly what is a human right, what are the sources of such rights, the priorities among them, and what protection should be given them. Religion has a large stake in pursuing this debate, but the diversity of religious ideas, especially across major cultural boundaries, is part of the problem. As noted earlier, current justifications of interventionary armed force appeal to only a minimal standard—gross violations of basic rights—as providing just cause for resort to such force. But if human rights are genuinely human, that is, common to all humankind, then surely much more could be done to expand the area of agreement as to such rights, and much more could be said about just which rights are worthy of protection in the international order. Since the conviction by the International Criminal Tribunal for the Former Yugoslavia of two men for enslaving enemy women for sexual purposes, there is a strong argument that protection against sexual assault has become a recognized "basic" right, alongside the right to such necessities as food, shelter, and medical care. This is still a very short, and very minimal, list. One may grant that not all human rights recognized in the various religious and cultural traditions of the world and in various international statements are equivalent in nature and deserve the same kind or degree of protection, and not all violations may justify resort to armed intervention to stop them. But there is no possibility of thinking coherently about this, of determining the level of protection due, unless we have a clearer and more common conception of the rights themselves. International agreements have helped to build confusion and disagreement by multiplying rights in different contexts; surely it is time to spend similar effort to the end of creating greater consensus, even if still only on the list of most basic rights, or those having the highest priority for international recognition and protection. Again, religious and moral discourse can make useful contributions to this effort.

Third, contemporary armed conflict has created a crisis in the law of war and in moral discourse on use of armed force by the systematic direct, intentional targeting of noncombatants as a means of making war. I am thinking here of a host of phenomena, of which the most flagrant examples include the Rwandan genocide, the ethnic cleansing of the wars of the former Yugoslavia, the amputation of hands and arms of ordinary civilians in Sierra Leone, and terrorist bombings in populated areas in the conflicts in Israel, Northern Ireland, and Sri Lanka. All these—genocide, ethnic cleansing, terrorism—are evil precisely in that they directly, intentionally attack people who have done nothing to deserve harm or death. I spoke earlier of the effort in some recent religious discourse to make the limits on harm to noncombatants even more restrictive. But the more fundamental moral problem posed by contemporary armed conflict is how to hold onto the consensus that is already there, which is incorporated in the international law on armed conflicts. This consensus has deep moral and religious roots, not only in the West but in other cultures. It has been spelled out in increasing detail in international law over the last 140 years. It has worked to limit and to stabilize armed conflict even in the most destructive wars of this period. Thus for it to be disregarded so frequently, so flagrantly, and so systematically in recent armed conflicts is a problem of very serious dimensions. I have suggested that a problem in the appeal to human rights when thinking about the justification of armed intervention in contemporary conflicts is that there is agreement on only the most basic rights. On the protection of noncombatants from direct, intentional attack there is, by contrast, a clear, consensually supported, highly institutionalized, and historically effective body of international law that, moreover, accords closely with moral tradition. So the problem here is different: it is how to hold on to that consensus and strengthen it in dealing with contemporary armed conflicts—and future ones.

Fourth, there is the problem of achieving the end of peace in practice. I have argued that peace should never be seen simply in terms of ending the fighting, but that achievement of peace requires the establishment of a just social and political order. This is also a central aim in recent religious discourse on dealing with conflict. As recent cases of humanitarian intervention have revealed, this is not an easy task to be performed quickly, but a complex one that requires many different kinds of resources and sustained effort over a significant period of time. Bosnia and Kosovo show what is needed: not just an end to the fighting but an ongoing presence of a military stabilization force, involvement by international agencies including the United Nations and regional organizations like the EU and OSCE, the presence of nongovernmental and private voluntary organizations over a sustained period of time, the building of institutional links with other societies to sustain peaceful stability once it is achieved. These two cases are models, but they are comparatively easy; other contemporary cases pose much more daunting challenges. If it is granted to be just, as I believe it is, for the United Nations, regional alliances, or even individual states in exceptional circumstances, to contemplate armed intervention in response to serious violations of human rights and/or the failure of states, then attention needs to be given in advance to what this implies after the intervention has taken place. That, in turn, means coming to terms with what is necessary to rebuild such societies after the fighting has been ended.

SECTION 3

FORCE AND CONFLICT

To date, we have looked at force as a malleable abstraction that can be pounded by the tenets of religion and pummeled by the law of nations without much regard for other influences on its ultimate shape. If we did not earlier recognize that we were incorrect, simply rereading the sentence above should persuade us that we were wrong. The primary purpose of the armed forces is to advance the interests of the political entity that has established them when these interests cannot be furthered by peaceful means; this requires that the limitations we seek to impose on their employment must either be consonant with this primary purpose or be so important that they justifiably override what would otherwise be deemed acceptable practices. We cannot look at all the situations where there may be a clash between politico-military requirements and ethical considerations but we will look at three of the most important, namely:

- The practice of statecraft, *i.e.*, the selection of the instruments and the policies by which a political entity seeks to advance its interests;
- The politics of war (or as Professor Albert Pierce terms it, "The Ethics of Strategy"): the guidelines covering the employment of the military instrument;
- The operational requirements stemming from the mission(s) of the armed forces.

Obviously, the role of statecraft, or diplomacy, is shaped partly by objective factors such as the nature of the international environment, the strengths of the major players, the level of military technology, etc., and partly by subjective ones, such as a country's definition of its national interests, the policies it adopts to further these, the resources it devotes to this task, and so on: in short, by its grand strategy. A definition of national interests which aims at maximizing power, and a set of policies which relies heavily on the military instrument for the promotion of these interests, will undoubtedly make different uses of force than one that has different objectives or a different view as to how to attain them. For instance, a state seeking to play a hegemonic role might tailor its armed forces to engage in preemption and war-fighting, one interested in maintaining the status quo might give priority to deterrence and one committed to conflict resolution might emphasize peacekeeping and humanitarian intervention.[1] Thus, as Ambassador James Goodby points out, the first step toward prescribing the role of force is the determination of a grand strategy, which will in turn affect the degree and nature of involvement in world affairs and the use of the military instrument.

Because of its implications, influencing the choice of a grand strategy is perhaps the most important task for religious people, religious organizations and all those concerned with laying out a peaceful path to a more peaceful world. Moreover, the issues to be resolved fall more directly within their spheres of interest and competence than do technical military matters. Furthermore, many of them are already engaged in promoting programs in economic and social development which hold some promise of reducing internal tensions and curbing resorts to violence, and hence have both knowledge of the situation and influence with those formulating and implementing national policy. To quote Ambassador Goodby, "There is a clear logic path between ethical norms, international rules of behavior, the rule of law, and the goals of U.S. diplomacy." At the very least religious groups should point out that path, as the Catholic Bishops Conference did in its statement of November 11, 1993,[2] and thereby help to create a just and stable peace.

Of course, even the best grand strategy designed cannot rule out the possibility of war; in fact, in some cases its effectiveness may depend on the use of force—albeit with some regard for ethical principles as well as for military objectives. Professor Pierce holds that the dichotomy between ethics and strategy may not be as marked as some would have us believe and makes his point by comparing "just war" guidelines with the strategic tenets of a seminal military thinker, General Karl von Clausewitz. Pierce noted that both "just cause" and Clausewitz's requirement that there be a valid political objective demonstrate that not all goals

---

1 These illustrations are drawn from Richard N. Haass' list of nine possible missions in *Using Force*, MANAGING GLOBAL CHAOS. (Crocker, Sampson & Aall eds., 1996).

- Deterrence, nuclear or conventional
- Preemption
- Peacekeeping
- War-fighting
- Nation-building
- Interdiction
- Humanitarian intervention
- Rescue missions.

To these might be added "compellence," *i.e.*, the attempt to induce another actor to alter its policy by the threat to employ force if it does not, and "coercion," the actual exercise of force for this purpose.

2 *See infra* Ch. 5.

of statecraft constitute legitimate reasons to go to war. He notes also that "probability of success" bears a striking resemblance to feasibility, as does proportionality to economy of force. Indeed, Pierce maintains that economy of force means that arms should not be turned against noncombatants nor used beyond the level required to achieve victory. All in all, the complementarity in principle between ethics and strategy suggests looking harder at how they can be jointly applied in practice—along with the guidelines derived from both international law and the military code of conduct.

This latter is no mean task. For one thing, as Professor Pierce acknowledges, judgments about "just cause," "valid political objective" and other criteria are essentially subjective and reasonable men can reasonably disagree as to their context. For another, in time of war men are not necessarily reasonable: they tend to dehumanize the enemy and to resort to fictions that obscure the true nature of their behavior, as Air Chief Marshal "Bomber" Harris did in counting walls knocked down in the British bombings of Hamburg and other German cities in WW II, and not the bodies buried beneath the rubble. Thus, both the psychology of war and its nature may militate against the kind of conduct that ethical principles would mandate.

General Andrew Goodpaster, in his chapter, took partial exception to this finding, calling on all protagonists—diplomats, officers, officials and religious leaders—to join in formulating a viable and acceptable approach for those occasions when the "problem is serious enough to require action but cannot be dealt with by means other than force."[3] To this end, he laid out a framework for analysis, understanding and decisionmaking in those cases involving the use of force, encompassing factors ranging from the causes of the conflict through the objectives to be achieved, the costs of so doing, the size, nature and organization of the force required to carry out the operation(s) and, above all, the command structure. His pithy conclusion was that "if war is too important to be entrusted to generals, it is too difficult to be entrusted to amateurs."[4]

If, as all agreed, we should try to factor into decisionmaking not only political guidance and operational requirements but legal constraints and ethical concerns, how can this be done? Obviously, the answer will differ according to the socio-cultural system and the political structure of the entity involved. In the case of the United States there are a number of possibilities, all of which aim at sensitizing participants to the ethical implications of what they propose to do. Some suggestions as to how to do this will be found in the three chapters, but essentially this is "unfinished business," whose completion is the task of all of us.

---

3 *See infra* CH. 7.

4 *Id.*

CHAPTER 5

PEACE, ETHICS AND THE USE OF FORCE

*James E. Goodby**

OVERVIEW

Peacekeeping, peacemaking, and humanitarian intervention are the most relevant uses of military force from the standpoint of the Program on Religion and Conflict Resolution, but there are many other security problems where force or the threat of force must be considered and these, also, have ethical components. The chief goal of the international community should be to prevent conflict situations from escalating into outright warfare; preventive diplomacy should ideally precede peacekeeping, peacemaking, and humanitarian intervention. Diplomacy and military force are two instruments of American statecraft that can be used for that purpose.

If the objective were simply to avoid situations where the use of U.S. military forces had to be contemplated, a grand strategy could be adopted by the United States to minimize U.S. involvement, even in cases where humanitarian intervention seemed warranted. Such doctrines would make U.S. involvement in peacekeeping and humanitarian interventions less likely although particular situations might be so clear-cut that a U.S. military intervention might be mounted despite the nation's grand strategy—U.S. neutrality in the period between World Wars I and II represented such a policy.

At the level of grand strategy, the reasons for war to occur could be removed thoroughly through appeasement, or through global or regional concerts that would foster restraint and accommodation. A grand strategy might stress the need for the international community to tackle peacekeeping, peacemaking, and humanitarian interventions more effectively, so that U.S. forces could be only minimally involved. An extreme example of deferring to others would amount to a disengagement strategy, this might save many U.S. casualties, but would be at the price of turning our backs on conflict resolution and peacemaking.

---

* Senior Fellow, The Brookings Institution.

Several elements of U.S. diplomacy could be combined in support of a grand strategy. Several of these elements could directly support conflict resolution (as opposed to management) and could be executed in the all-important preventive diplomacy mode.

A U.S. grand strategy most conducive to preventing conflict or, if necessary, for implementing peacekeeping, peacemaking, or humanitarian intervention operations would include elements of devolution, global or regional concerts, and delegation to international organizations. It is a basic rule of international life that early engagement in conflict prevention by the United States is necessary to minimize levels of violence.

USE OF FORCE

Uses of force in statecraft were categorized neatly by Richard N. Haass.[1]

- Deterrence—Usually thought of as nuclear, deterrence applies to all forms of threats of punishments directed at preventing certain actions by other nations. An example is the threat issued by the George H. W. Bush administration against Saddam Hussein to the effect that his use of weapons of mass destruction would result in major damage to his own country.
- Preemption—This is the idea that a developing threat to international security might be attacked in order to prevent the emergence of that threat. A case in point is the Israeli attack against an Iraqi nuclear reactor several years ago. President George W. Bush has stated that this will be the policy the U.S. military will use against terrorist threats.
- Peacekeeping—This form of use of force has been associated primarily with UN operations, but NATO and the European Union have begun to conduct such operations in the Balkans. Peacekeeping usually involves an agreement by parties to a conflict that they will enter into a ceasefire observed by military forces sent under international auspices.
- War-fighting—The use of force by national governments, either to defend against aggression, or to impose the national will on another country. The U.S. war in Afghanistan fits this category since the Taliban government in Afghanistan gave sanctuary to al-Qaida even after September 11.
- Peacemaking—The use of force to impose a peace or a cease-fire on parties to a conflict. In recent years peacemaking has been used for intrastate conflicts although not exclusively so. Chapter 7 of the UN charter provides that the Security Council can author-

---

1 *Using Force, in* MANAGING GLOBAL CHAOS (Crocker, Sampson, & Aall eds. 1996). His typology will be followed here.

ize forces to stop a conflict even over the opposition of parties to the conflict. An example was the use of military forces to expel Iraq from Kuwait, in that case an interstate conflict.

- Nation-building—Often misinterpreted, this term implies broader actions than just the use of force. However, when force is used as a part of a nation-building effort, it is usually aimed at creating conditions of relative peace to permit the strengthening of civil institutions. The U.S. involvement in Afghanistan has developed into a type of nation-building effort.
- Interdiction—This term refers to the use of military force to stop a specific action by an adversary. Interdiction was used in Bosnia on occasion by the UN and NATO forces to prevent Serb attacks on Muslim-inhabited cities. The massacre at Srebeniza showed the limitations of inadequately supported interdiction operations
- Humanitarian intervention—This applies to the use of force to prevent attacks on a particular population, usually by the government in control of the area inhabited by that population. A classic case was NATO's intervention to prevent the expulsion of the Albanian Kosovars from Kosovo.
- Rescue missions—This applies to the use of military forces to extricate endangered populations from a threatening situation. These threatening situations can include civil wars, as in several countries in Africa, or natural disasters. An example is the use of military forces to assist the victims of earthquakes and floods, as in Bangladesh.

POLICIES GOVERNING THE USE OF MILITARY FORCE

Such policies can be defined in a "top down" sense, that is, imposed by the U.S. president. In this case, these policies are likely to form part of a grand strategy. John Lewis Gaddis,[2] compared Eisenhower's nuclear deterrent strategy and Kennedy's strategy of countering threats directly with U.S. military force. He concludes that Eisenhower's policies resulted in less involvement of U.S. forces in small wars. The Weinberger/Powell doctrine during the Reagan and Bush administrations also imposed conditions that in principle reduced the frequency of U.S. military involvement.

Policies concerning the use of military force also can be constructed in a "bottom up" sense, that is, individual specific issues can affect military strategy. Such pragmatic decisionmaking usually hinges on the availability of military forces. If U.S. military forces have as their chief priority the goals of deterrence and defense against massive attack, there could be situations where there are no forces left over for humanitarian interventions

---

2 STRATEGIES OF CONTAINMENT (1982).

or peacekeeping. Or, at the other extreme, if the principal threat to international peace and security appeared to come from intrastate conflicts or terrorism, the U.S. military could be spread very thin, with few resources available for unforeseen contingencies. Such dilemmas appear to be exactly what is frustrating NATO. NATO's mission, as seen by the United States, has changed from an emphasis on defense against aggression to the need to project force beyond Europe.

GRAND STRATEGY

American presidents can adopt grand strategies that would affect preventive diplomacy as well as peacekeeping, peacemaking, and humanitarian intervention, quite decisively. The following list illustrates the point:

A. Hegemony, imposed unilaterally if necessary. The United States has unparalleled military power and should use it to arrange a world congenial to U.S. interests. This includes "regime change" through force where other alternatives are not available.[3]

B. Devolution.[4] The U.S. recedes from hegemon role, encouraging others to take up the burdens. The structure of international relations can contribute to peace and more reliance would be placed on multilateral efforts to deal with conflict.

C. Global or regional concerts. Restraint and accommodation, perhaps with some acknowledgement of spheres of interest, among the globe's power centers.[5] Peacekeeping, peacemaking, and humanitarian intervention may be handled better on a regional basis than on a global basis.

D. Delegation. Reliance on international organizations, perhaps a standing UN military force or an international police force. This would be a desirable option for peacekeeping, peacemaking, and humanitarian intervention if the United States really got behind it.

E. Appeasement.[6] This policy brings to mind Hitler and Chamberlain but there are circumstances where appeasement is a desirable policy. An example is the British decision not to try to counter the rising naval power of the United States in the 19th century. A more modest idea—accommodation—may help to prevent unnecessary conflicts.

---

[3] *See* the writings of Kristol, Kagan, Kraathammer, and Perle for examples of the argument in *Present Dangers: Crisis and Opportunity in American Foreign Policy and Defense Policy*. Eds. Robert Kagan and William Kristol. Encounter Books: (March 2000.)

[4] *See* Charles Kupchan, *After Pax Americana*, INTERNATIONAL SECURITY (Fall 1998.)

[5] *See* JAMES E. GOODBY, EUROPE UNDIVIDED (1998).

[6] *See* Alexander George, *Appeasement as a Strategy for Conflict Avoidance, in* BRIDGING THE GAP, (1993).

F. Disengagement.[7] This could apply especially to intrastate conflicts and would most likely lead to a hands-off approach by the United States.

The Diplomacy of Grand Strategies

Each of these grand strategies except for the first—hegemony—would rely more on diplomacy than on military force. For example:

A. Less reliance on coercive diplomacy, more reliance on incentives.[8]
B. A higher premium on skillful execution of preventive diplomacy.[9]
C. Clearer definition of core interests.[10]
D. More support for international organizations.
E. Unilateralism reserved for exceptional situations.
F. More attention to conflict resolution.[11]

Assessment and Illustration of Strategies

None of the grand strategies mentioned above, in its pure form, would serve U.S. interests. Elements of several would be necessary to form a successful strategy. Lessons of the past suggest that:

- Postponing intervention may result ultimately in higher levels of violence.
- Engagement, rather than disengagement, is likely to forestall escalation of conflicts to the most intense levels of violence.
- Preventive diplomacy is needed to defuse conflicts and this must begin many years before conflicts erupt into violence, and continue so long as the potential for conflict exists.

Examples of Statecraft in Regional Conflicts

A strategy that encourages U.S. engagement in regional issues to prevent conflict is the first step. Taking Korea as an illustration of this point, the United States should have a proactive strategy aimed at a gradual reconciliation between North and South Korea. This proactive strategy has a military component, consisting of the forward deployment of U.S. forces

---

7 *See* a series of CATO Institute papers, such as *Death Knell for NATO: The Bush Administration Confronts the European Security and Defense Policy*. Layne, Christopher. CATO Policy Analysis No. 394. (April 2, 2001).

8 *See* ALEXANDER GEORGE, FORCEFUL PERSUASION (1991).

9 *See* Barry M. Blechman & Tamara Cofman Wittes, *Defining Moment: The Threat and Use of Force in American Foreign Policy Since 1989, in* INTERNATIONAL CONFLICT RESOLUTION AFTER THE COLD WAR (Paul C. Stern & Daniel Druckman eds., 2000).

10 *See* James E. Goodby, *Collective Security in Europe After the Cold War*, J. INT'L. AFFAIRS (1993).

11 *See International Conflict Resolution After the Cold War.*

in and around Korea. This is aimed at assuring South Koreans that their security is being attended to, and that they can go about the business of building a successful civil society. It is also directed at deterring North Korea from any serious consideration of an armed attack on South Korea.

There must also be a diplomatic component in such a strategy. A proactive U.S. preventive diplomacy should include support for South Korea's engagement policies with the North, as well as appropriate levels of U.S. engagement with North Korea. The objective, of course, is to encourage a "soft landing" by absorbing North Korea into regional and global economic transactions and eventually into confederation with the Republic of Korea.

Given limited resources available to the United States, such preventive diplomacy is necessary to ensure the availability of U.S. forces for participation in humanitarian operations when these become necessary.

The case of Kosovo is an excellent illustration of the need for a U.S. strategy, supported by military and diplomatic efforts, that encourages other nations to work with us in multilateral coalitions to conduct humanitarian interventions. Coercive diplomacy was used against the Milosevic government to oblige that government to cease military operations against the Albanian Kosovars. Russia, which is an interested party in the Balkans, supported diplomatic efforts to persuade Milosevic not to use force, but refused to agree that the principle of sovereignty should be undercut by any external use of force against Yugoslavia. A UN Security Council resolution endorsing intervention would have been vetoed by Russia and probably by China. NATO intervened, under the leadership of the United States, without the benefit of a new UN Security Council resolution. The intervention was successful, but it left a bitter residue of anti-U.S. feeling in Russia and elsewhere.

It also led to U.S. disenchantment with the role of NATO in such interventions and probably to the decline of NATO as an effective military organization. The incident shows, however, that the United States needs to have a strategy that encourages big power cooperation in intrastate conflicts, and that provides for the use of international forces that might not include the United States military.

A More "Humble" US Foreign Policy[12]

Only policies of strategic restraint and accommodation, where possible, will facilitate understandings with the big powers when the need for humanitarian interventions arises. Furthermore, since the use of U.S. military forces can be misinterpreted as an attempt by the United States to acquire privileged positions, U.S. strategy should be directed at strength-

[12] Borrowed from a phrase used by President G. W. Bush.

ening regional conflict resolution, peacekeeping, peacemaking, and humanitarian intervention capabilities.

The decision of the Bush administration to terminate the "Two War" requirement for U.S. military forces is a very good example of how policies can be put in place that would release U.S. military assets for use in humanitarian interventions. This will be helpful in adjusting U.S. contributions to NATO to meet new military requirements which, in the European region, focus mainly on peacemaking and humanitarian intervention. The President's preemption strategy, however, is a step in the opposite direction. We should take care to avoid too prominent a role for U.S. military forces in the future.

RELEVANCE OF CORE RELIGIOUS VALUES TO STRATEGIC CHOICES

The involvement of religious people and religious organizations in mediating or resolving intrastate ethnic or communal conflict has proven its worth and is now well established. Such involvement offers a more holistic approach to dealing with conflicts than governments by themselves can provide. Religious groups, however, have not been as seriously involved in choices about U.S. national strategies as their values and sense of responsibility suggest they should be. A partial exception to this is the U.S. Catholic Bishops Pastoral letter on war and peace, 20 years ago.

There is a clear logic path between ethical norms, international rules of behavior, the rule of law, and the goals of U.S. diplomacy. This logic path is generally ignored by religious organizations, which have been focused on tactical rather than strategic issues. A systemic bias against involvement by religious groups at that level of national discourse apparently exists. This could involve religious groups in the policymaking process, an involvement which many groups, quite rightly, think is inappropriate, given the separation of church and state in the United States. Nonetheless, most religious groups probably can agree that the use of force is to be avoided, wherever possible, and that the United States should have a leading role in order-building diplomacy, aimed at reducing the likelihood of armed struggle. The term "cathedral building" is a good metaphor for this.

A special American contribution to international relations has been the effort, generally associated with Woodrow Wilson, to inject an element of morality and the rule of law into the domain of interstate relations. Realists consider that this whole idea is out of keeping with the amoral behavior of states in the international system, but the tradition of the rule of law as a component of international relations runs very deep in American society. At the very least, it should be possible for religious groups to insist that military power, and the use of force, could be tempered and balanced by U.S. policies aimed at creating a stable peace, to which an international order that accords real weight to the rule of law could make a significant contribution.

Religious groups could also be engaged in helping to define criteria for collective military intervention. Governments tend to consider intervention from the standpoint of whether there is a potential for wider conflict, or whether the survival of a friendly, and in our case, a democratic, government is at stake. Governments also are preoccupied by the effect of a conflict on international norms, particularly those related to the use of force to change established frontiers. Religious groups, on the other hand, may be equally concerned with other principles, such as those affecting human rights. Religious groups also should have a voice in determining that one of the criteria for armed intervention should be based on moral considerations, such as whether crimes against humanity are being committed. Collective security requires that governments perceive that a flouting of broadly accepted international norms is a direct threat to their national interests, even though their own interests may not be immediately affected. In making judgments of this kind, governments need to and ought to have the perspective of citizens viewing these issues from the standpoint of religious values. These examples strongly suggest that there is an important role for religious people and religious groups, not only at the grass roots level of conflict, but also at the level of broad national policymaking.

CHAPTER 6

CONFLICT, STRATEGY, AND ETHICS

*Dr. Albert C. Pierce**

INTRODUCTION

The conference organizers asked me to focus my chapter on outside intervention, especially by the United States, in intrastate conflict, including civil wars, genocide, and ethnic cleansing.[1] This guidance usefully narrows the assignment, and frees me from having to address issues of interstate conflict. At the same time, I choose to narrow it further by not extensively addressing important aspects—international law, grand strategy, and military operations—discussed elsewhere at the conference and in this book by experts whose knowledge and experience in these fields dwarf my own. Thus I address grand strategy and military operations along the way in this chapter, trying to complement the more thorough consideration Ambassador James E. Goodby and General Andrew Goodpaster, respectively, give them. In the case of international law, I do not address it at all, as Professor James Turner Johnson has done so admirably and authoritatively in his chapter. Rather my chapter addresses the middle level between grand strategy and military operations.

I've organized this chapter in three parts. First, I will address strategy and ethics, in particular how both can, and often do, point in the same direction—towards placing limits on conflicts, including both wars and humanitarian interventions. Second, I will highlight a contemporary phenomenon in humanitarian intervention that troubles me—casualty aversion —and examine how that phenomenon runs counter to both strategy and ethics. Third, I will offer some thoughts on contributions that could or should be made by religion and religious organizations to the above cluster of topics.

---

* Director, Center for the Study of Professional Military Ethics, USNA.

1 "Ethnic cleansing" is a current term of art. I use it only because everyone else does, but I don't like it. The reason I don't like it is that I've never been able to figure out just who or what is "cleansed" by ethnic cleansing.

STRATEGY AND ETHICS

These subjects are generally seen as two quite separate domains, two bodies of literature, two logics, two languages, worked by two quite separate groups of people, often for quite different purposes. The conventional wisdom has it that these two domains are in some necessary and fundamental tension, even direct conflict, with each other. My thesis is that not only are they are not necessarily in tension and are certainly not fundamentally opposed to each other, but also that they can, and often do, point in the same direction—towards placing limits on conflict.

Here, I would split a strategic and ethical hair with Dr. Donald W. Shriver, Jr., who argues in his chapter that "there is a tension between the military objective of winning the war as quickly as possible, and with the fewest possible deaths among the members of the armed services, and the moral objective of limiting the destruction of life and property."[2] My own view is that while there sometimes might be such a tension, there is no necessary tension between the two.

Strategy and ethics can, in certain circumstances, be mutually reinforcing. They can, and often do, place limits on both the resort to military force and on how military force is used, in humanitarian interventions as well as in war.

Let me briefly review key concepts from these two literatures, languages, and logics. My own thinking about strategy and ethics goes back to a 19th-century Prussian officer and a fifth-century African saint—Carl von Clausewitz and Augustine.

Strategy

In his classic treatise, *On War*, Clausewitz says that "...war is an act of force and there is no logical limit to the application of that force."[3] There is no place for half measures in war: "To introduce the principle of moderation into the theory of war would always lead to a logical absurdity."[4] For Clausewitz, war involves powerful emotions, among the most powerful in human experience, and these emotions tend to drive war out of control.

But Clausewitz goes on to point out that war in practice seldom looks like war in theory as he has presented it. There are many reasons why, but one is especially relevant for our present purposes—Clausewitz's Trinity:

> As a total phenomenon [war's] dominant tendencies always make it a remarkable trinity—composed of primordial violence, hatred,

---

2 *See supra* Ch. 3.

3 CARL VON CLAUSEWITZ, ON WAR 77 (Michael Howard & Peter Paret eds. & trans., 1976).

4 *Id.* at 76.

> and enmity, which are to be regarded as a blind natural force; of the play of chance and probability within which the creative spirit is free to roam; and of its element of subordination, as an instrument of policy, which makes it subject to reason alone.[5]

(I believe that here, as with much of what Clausewitz writes, we can generalize from what he says about war to other forms of conflict, including humanitarian intervention. Thus, whenever Clausewitz uses the word "war," one can substitute "any use of military force," and his message generally still applies.)

It is this third part of his trinity, "the political aims [which] are the business of government alone,"[6] that drives towards limits in war. For Clausewitz, war is governed by its political objectives:

> No one starts a war—or rather, no one in his senses ought to do so—without first being clear in his mind what he intends to achieve by that war and how he intends to conduct it. The former is its [political objective]; the latter is its [military objective]. This is the governing principle which will set its course, prescribe the scale of means and effort which is required, and make its influence felt down to the smallest operational detail.[7]

The political objectives drive everything else. The political objective "is the goal, war is the means of reaching it, and means can never be considered in isolation from their purpose."[8] Political objectives, of course, vary greatly, some being geo-strategic in origin, others ideological or even religious in nature. But in all cases, *strategy* takes the political objectives and ensures that the military operations are conducted so as to accomplish those objectives—and only those objectives.

For Clausewitz, war must always be proportionate to its political objectives: Total political objectives lead to total war, and limited political objectives lead to limited war. Setting political objectives is the function of government. Far more often than not, government establishes limited political objectives, so most wars are—and should be—limited wars, and by extension, most humanitarian interventions are—and should be—limited interventions.

Clausewitz says the strategist should "act on the principle of using no greater force, and setting himself no greater military aim, than would be sufficient for the achievement of his political purpose."[9] This echoes one of the traditional military principles of war, economy of force.

---

5 *Id.* at 89.

6 *Id.*

7 *Id.* at 579.

8 *Id.* at 87.

9 *Id.* at 585.

There have been references by other presenters to the contemporary concept of "overwhelming force." In my own view, overwhelming force does not necessarily contradict economy of force. The latter says that one should use only as much force as is needed to achieve the objectives, an essentially Clausewitzian principle. In some circumstances, decisive or overwhelming force might be able to achieve the objectives more quickly, even at less loss of life, than smaller amounts of force applied more slowly over time. Of course, overwhelming force can also lead to excessive force, but my point here is that there is no necessary contradiction between overwhelming force and economy of force. Economy of force is a relative proposition, not an absolute one—relative to the objective to be accomplished. And for Clausewitz, it is the government, the policy-makers, who set the objectives, which ultimately determine the force requirements.

For Clausewitz, the relationship is clear:

> Since war is not an act of senseless passion, but is controlled by its political object[ive], the value of this object[ive] must determine the sacrifices to be made for it in magnitude and also in duration. Once the expenditure of effort exceeds the value of the political object[ive], the object[ive] must be renounced and peace must follow.[10]

That is a stern caution from a 19th-century Prussian officer. And it runs counter to a line more familiar to most readers, "There is no substitute for victory." General Douglas MacArthur had a very different concept of war than did Clausewitz, at least on this point.

"Warfare," Clausewitz writes, "thus eludes the strict requirement that extremes of force be applied."[11] This is true of any type of military operation, including humanitarian intervention. Military operations can, and should be, limited so as to serve the particular political objectives set by government policy. There is a standard against which the conduct of military operations should be measured—the political objectives—and there is someone responsible for limiting it—political leadership.

Strategy, then, is a demanding taskmaster, and it runs counter to some of our most basic and powerful emotions. Strategy can usefully be thought of as the art and science of how government and its policy wrestle to the ground "primordial violence, hatred, and enmity" on the battlefield, in higher headquarters, in the halls of decisionmaking, and especially among the people. Strategy makes the use of military force purposeful. It channels it, constrains it, limits it.

---

10 *Id.* at 92.

11 *Id.* at 80.

Ethics

If the Clausewitz strategy is the effort to prevail over primordial violence, hatred, and enmity, then for Augustine and his religious successors in the just war tradition, perhaps ethics is the effort to prevail over the effects of original sin, including tendencies towards aggression. I draw on the just war principles here because it is the dominant tradition in the West regarding the ethical criteria for resort to and employment of military force.

The just war tradition includes religious roots, to be sure, but as James Turner Johnson has demonstrated, it also has roots in philosophy, the law, the practice of statecraft, and military codes. So while religious leaders are not its sole custodians, they are among its primary custodians. The just war tradition is part of the Western heritage, though much of what it contains is reflected in other religious traditions' thinking on war. Here too, Professor Johnson is among the most respected scholars. To be sure, not all religious traditions or cultures invoke the just war, but discussion of it is directly relevant when talking about U.S. strategy and military operations because the United States is firmly anchored in the Western tradition, which includes the just war. Our enemies or adversaries may or may not adhere to this tradition, but we generally do and always should.

As has already been elaborated by Professor Johnson and by Dr. Shriver, the just war principles are divided into two parts—the *jus ad bellum*, which governs the decision to go to war (or to commit military forces), and the *jus in bello*, which governs the conduct of war (or other military operations). In this chapter, let me highlight how these two sets of criteria serve to limit either the resort to force or the use of force once committed, all in parallel to how strategy can point towards similar limits. Although the just war criteria apply to all forms of conflict, I will focus here on humanitarian intervention, not on interstate conflict.

The list of *jus ad bellum* criteria generally begins with "just cause." This criterion says that not all objectives set by political leaders are legitimate reasons for going to war. There have been considerable debates throughout the history of the just war tradition about what does, and what does not, constitute just cause, and the generally accepted causes have changed over time as well. But at no point in the history of the tradition has any responsible person said that any and all objectives set by political leaders are just causes for using military force. Just cause itself drives towards limits.

In the contemporary debate over humanitarian intervention, not even those with the most expansive views on what constitutes legitimate reasons for intervention believe that all humanitarian crises qualify as just causes. The so-called Realist-Cosmopolitan debate is over just how serious or severe the crisis has to be—and for the Realists it must threaten vital U.S. national interests—for it to be an acceptable reason, politically or ethically, to intervene.

Just cause serves to limit humanitarian interventions in another way, *i.e.*, by limiting the scope of the objective. In most interventions, the just cause is stated negatively, for example, to prevent or to stop genocide or ethnic cleansing, rather than positively, *i.e.*, to build a peaceful, functioning society in the target country. While in a larger sense, the intervention to stop the killing may point towards an "ultimate peace," rare is the intervention that aims to accomplish that just, though ambitious objective. Here, too, ethics finds mutual reinforcement in strategy, for rarely does political leadership, certainly in the United States, buy into the "in-for-a-dime, in-for-a-dollar" proposition—nor, for that matter, does the public.

And, of course, since the *jus ad bellum* requires that all five criteria be met, even the most cosmopolitan of the cosmopolitans accept the notion that just cause is not sufficient, that the other, pragmatic criteria must be met as well. In this sense, just war is both an ethic of intentions and an ethic of consequences.

A second *jus ad bellum* criterion that has been central in the debates over humanitarian intervention is "competent authority." The traditional interpretation is that only the duly constituted civil authorities of the state have the authority to enter into war, or to commit military forces.

In the past decade or so, one question that has been debated is whether for humanitarian interventions, as opposed to cases of cross-border aggression or interstate conflict, any one state constitutes competent authority, and therefore whether some form of multilateral authorization ought to be required. The argument put forward by advocates of multilateral authorization is usually based on a desire to resist, or at least reduce, the temptations of the powerful to intervene in the affairs of smaller states. A more sophisticated version of the multilateral authorization school distinguishes between authorization and execution, arguing that multilateral authorization does not necessarily imply or require multilateral execution, thus taking into account the inherent complexities and the spotty track record of interventions by multinational forces.

A third criterion of *jus ad bellum* that has played an important role in policy debates about humanitarian interventions is "probability of success," the traditional interpretation of which is that one may resort to war, or the use of force, only if there is a reasonable chance of achieving the just cause that motivates the war (or humanitarian intervention). Put another way, probability of success says that only a reasonable chance of achieving the good of the war can justify the inevitable costs and harm that will be done, intentionally and unintentionally, through the employment of military force. Military strategists are talking about the same factor when they speak of "feasibility." Here the strategic and the ethical vocabularies are different, but the concepts are the same. In humanitarian interventions the debate has almost a perverse twist, *i.e.*, that the more horrible the humanitarian crisis, the more it constitutes just cause, but also the less likely that outsiders can make a major, let alone a lasting, difference for the good.

A fourth criterion that enters into the humanitarian intervention debate is "proportionality," which says that the harm that will result, intentionally and unintentionally, from a military operation should not be disproportionate to the good that will be accomplished.

In contemporary policy discussions, a seemingly related military concept—overwhelming force or decisive force—often is introduced, and the argument is made that overwhelming force inevitably violates proportionality. Thus any military operation involving overwhelming force, so the argument goes, cannot pass all six of the *jus ad bellum* criteria. My own view is quite different. The just war criterion of proportionality has to do with the ratio of outcomes—harm done vs. good accomplished. The military concept of overwhelming force, in contrast, has to do with the ratio of inputs, *i.e.*, the force balance between the two sides. Thus the two are not inherently contradictory; proportionality does not necessarily rule out overwhelming force, in war or in humanitarian interventions. Applying overwhelming force can, of course, violate proportionality, but that depends on how the force is used, against whom and what, rather than on the ratio of forces itself.

A fifth *jus ad bellum* criterion—last resort—also plays a role in debates over humanitarian interventions. The traditional interpretation of this prudential criterion is that one ought to try other, nonviolent means of resolving disputes before turning to the bloody military instrument. It is a prudential, not an absolute requirement: No responsible commentator has argued that a nation under armed attack may not fight back until it has exhausted nonviolent means of stopping the invasion.

In many debates over humanitarian interventions during the 1990s, this issue was posed as military interventions vs. economic sanctions. I have argued elsewhere[12] that in some instances, such as the humanitarian crisis in Haiti in the early 1990s, a moral argument can be made for an early, surgical military intervention to overthrow a cruel regime inflicting massive suffering on its people rather than relying first on broad-brush economic sanctions, the net effect of which is more often than not to inflict additional suffering on the miserable populations.

---

12 Albert C. Pierce, *Just War Principles and Economic Sanctions*, 10 ETHICS & INT'L AFFAIRS 99–113 (1996).

Let me turn now to the second set of just war criteria—the *jus in bello*—which govern the conduct of war or other military operations. Here there are two—discrimination and proportionality.

The just war requires discrimination between combatants and noncombatants. The underlying principle is noncombatant immunity, which says that noncombatants may never be the object of a deliberately intended attack. It does not say that non-combatants may never be killed, but rather that they may not be the object of an attack. It thus recognizes that accidents and unintentional harm to noncombatants do happen in war. Discrimination is an ethic of intention.

The challenges to discrimination and to noncombatant immunity in humanitarian interventions are well known, not only to soldiers and policymakers, but to the public as well, especially since the publication of the book *Black Hawk Down*[13] and the release of the movie by the same name. But discrimination still serves to drive towards limits in how force is applied, even in humanitarian interventions.

Proportionality in *jus in bello* reflects the same underlying principle of proportionality in *jus ad bellum, i.e.*, that the harm done may not outweigh the good that is accomplished. The difference is that in the *jus in bello*, one is measuring the harm and the good to be done by a particular military operation, not the overall war. Here too, *Black Hawk Down* is rich in case-study material.

Taken together, discrimination and proportionality provide considerable protection for noncombatants from much of the harm they would no doubt otherwise suffer in war and in humanitarian interventions. Here, too, strategy and ethics point in the same direction. Michael Walzer says that *jus in bello* imposes "an economy of force. It requires discipline and calculation. Any intelligent military strategy, of course, imposes the same requirement." One might also see the *jus in bello* as consistent with Clausewitz's admonition that "once the expenditure of effort exceeds the value of the political object[ive], the object[ive] must be renounced and peace must follow."

The bottom line in this first part of my chapter is that strategy and ethics can and often do both drive towards limits, and may indeed be quite mutually reinforcing—and that they are not in any fundamental, necessary tension or conflict. There is wisdom in using both logics, and not just one. What we need if we are to be successful at this very difficult business is statesmen, military commanders, and citizens who are, if not fluent in, at least conversant with both languages.

---

13 Mark Bowden, Black Hawk Down, (2000).

CASUALTY AVERSION

This contemporary phenomenon goes by several names—casualty aversion, zero military casualties (on our side!), and radical force protection, among them. I use the first, but whatever you call it, my thesis is that this phenomenon runs almost diametrically counter to central concepts of both strategy and ethics. It has occurred most commonly in humanitarian interventions, in which the argument is often made that the stakes themselves, which do not touch vital national interests, do not warrant the loss of the lives of friendly troops. Though, as I will elaborate below, it involves stakes of arguably marginal (for the Americans) strategic merit but considerable moral weight, I will use the 1999 war over Kosovo as a case in point. It is, in important ways, the defining case.

What was the moral problem with NATO's war in Kosovo? Before the moral analysis, of course, comes observation and the empirical analysis. I begin my analysis of the Kosovo war with NATO's stated political objective, which was to prevent genocide or, at a minimum, massive ethnic cleansing.

But, I would argue, the desire to keep friendly military casualties at or near zero led NATO chose to design a military strategy that: (1) did not include a ground invasion, (2) did not include even a plausible threat of a ground invasion, and (3) kept Allied pilots flying above 15,000 feet. These three factors combined to yield a strategy that, I would argue, was incapable of achieving the stated political objective.

The problem was that the damage being inflicted on and threatened against the Kosovar Albanians was being perpetrated by small, widely dispersed groups of Serbs, who were almost immune to the kind of air attacks NATO conducted. Strategically, the point of a ground threat was that it might well force the Serbs to mass in order to defend themselves, and by massing to become more vulnerable to air attack, especially if NATO were willing to fly lower so as to engage directly the fighting forces in the field. With no NATO threat from the ground, the Serbs could—and did—remain scattered and thus safe from NATO air attacks and free to continue their onslaught. (As it turned out, the damage the Serbs inflicted, horrible though it was, was not as great as had been feared or as it could have been, but luck is not proof of NATO strategic brilliance or moral courage.) Thus the strategy NATO chose failed, in my judgment at least, the just war criterion of probability of success. Another military, political, and moral consequence of this strategy was, of course, that NATO bombed many so-called "dual-use" targets (bridges, power facilities, and so forth), the loss of which had adverse effects not only on the Serbian armed forces and government, but also on civilian noncombatants.

So what began as a war to prevent genocide became a war to reverse the effects of the massive damage the Serbs were able to perpetrate against the Kosovars—damage that another, more risky, more costly strategy might have prevented, or at least significantly reduced. NATO tolerated this destruction, while deploring it, in order to keep friendly military casualties at or near zero.

From the perspective of strategy, zero military casualties appears to optimize for means over ends, to make ends secondary to means, indeed even to absolutize for means. In Kosovo, where the end was to prevent genocide, the strategy focused on means in terms of trying to hold our casualties at or near zero. From the perspective of ethics, zero military casualties seems to place a greater premium, and perhaps even a greater moral worth, on the lives of our own combatants than on the lives of innocent victims.

Let me overstate the point to make a point: In Kosovo, what NATO seemed to be implying in its deeds, though of course not in its words, was that preventing genocide and massive ethnic cleansing was not worth the lives of even a few NATO troops, that the lives of all the Kosovars were not worth the lives of even a couple of NATO pilots.

If the stakes in Kosovo—preventing genocide or massive ethnic cleansing—did not, in the eyes of many, warrant loss of the lives of friendly forces, then what can, has been, and will be said about humanitarian crises that do not rise to the level of genocide or ethnic cleansing?

Perhaps religious communities can contribute to this discussion, since most of them have threads in their traditions that have to do with sacrificing, even oneself, for the other and for the greater good. This last point leads easily to the third part of my paper.

CONTRIBUTIONS OF AND BY RELIGION

The conference organizers asked me to make some comments on the role religion can and does play in these areas. I believe religion can make contributions to debate and decisionmaking here on at least two levels. The first is the personal religious convictions of political leaders, military commanders, opinionmakers, and other elites, as they participate in the wide-ranging and messy process of policymaking and implementation in democratic societies. The second level is that of religious communities, principally through their leaders and organizational structures, but also their adherents as well. As interest groups and as citizens, people of religious faith have a legitimate role to play in these processes, consistent of course with our Constitutional provisions on church and state. I can identify several ways in which religious beliefs and people of faith can affect the issues we have been discussing. One is about process, the others about substance.

The process point is a small but important one, in my view. As military commanders make strategic and tactical decisions about the use of military force, they take ethical issues into account. The principal vehicle they employ is legal advice from their military lawyers, whose expertise on the law of war and the law of armed conflict is brought to bear regularly, indeed frequently, on decisions as specific as choice of weapons and targets. Some, myself included, argue that, as valuable and even essential as this legal advice is, it is too narrow, and that commanders would benefit from advice on the ethical dimensions of their work from other sources, perhaps including chaplains. There is anecdotal evidence that some senior officers do avail themselves of ideas and advice from chaplains, though this is usually done quite informally and intermittently.

Providing this kind of advice more regularly and systematically would require chaplains to educate themselves more than they generally do about both strategy and their own religious traditions' principles on war, the use of military force, and violence. Very few chaplains attend the most senior U.S. military schools, the war colleges, all of which provide substantial course work in strategy and strategic thinking. Chaplains are generally trained and focused on their pastoral work, not matters of substantive ethical dimensions of military strategy and operations. Thus, if they were to play this sort of augmented role, the chaplains corps in the various services would have to send more of their members to war colleges and command-and-staff colleges, and they would have to include more formal instruction in their own chaplains' courses on the just war and other religious traditions related to war and armed conflict.

There is some evidence of progress. The U.S. Navy's Chaplains School has taken a significant step in this direction, by instituting, in 2000, a new course for senior chaplains, in which one half day has been devoted to the discussion of war, strategy, and ethics. In July 2002, I will conduct such a seminar for the third straight year.

Of course, the same advice works in the opposite direction, *i.e.*, that the service academies, command-and-staff colleges, and war colleges could and should institute more courses on religion and conflict. The professional military education institutions are, to be sure, not alone or unique in paying systematic attention to the roles that religion can and does play in conflict and conflict prevention. The broader academic community, in particular the security studies and international relations programs and scholars, has only in the last decade begun to pay serious attention to religion as an empirical factor, if not a normative factor.[14]

More broadly, ethical considerations (though not necessarily religiously motivated) could be woven into military exercises and training, so that soldiers and their officers would have opportunity to think through these complex issues and how they present themselves in classroom and

---

[14] The path-breaking book in this field, in the eyes of many, myself included, was Religion, the Missing Dimension of Statecraft, (Douglas Johnston & Cynthia Sampson, 1994).

field-training scenarios before they encounter them in the real-world situations. This goal is implicit in the mission of the Center I direct: "To promote and enhance the ethical development of current and future military leaders through education, research, and reflection." Much of our work reaches out beyond the classrooms and walls of the Naval Academy into the classrooms and field training of various Navy and Marine Corps schools, and we aim to do even more.

On substance, I would suggest that religious communities, or those parts of them that address these sorts of issues, engage on the question I alluded to earlier—the issue of last resort in humanitarian crises in which policymakers are confronted with a choice between economic sanctions and the use of military force. Those religious leaders usually most active in such issues tend, far more often than not, to emphasize the traditional just war concept of last resort, interpreted quite literally and narrowly, *i.e.*, that governments ought to exhaust nonviolent means before turning to the military instrument.

Some substantial re-thinking along the lines I suggested in the first part of this paper should be encouraged. Religious leaders should give focused thought to whether their tradition does and should focus more on the kind of instrument to use (military force or economic sanctions) or on who suffers (the ruling elite or the population). I have argued elsewhere[15] that one ought to broaden the concept of harm, which in just war traditionally focuses on weapons that kill, to look at other ways that people can be seriously harmed, for example, by sanctions that, in intention and in effect, deprive powerless populations of goods they are already direly short of, and do not have similar adverse effects on wealthy influential elites who have numerous opportunities to "work around" the restrictions imposed by economic sanctions.

More broadly, religious leaders should probe their traditions on the issue of which humanitarian crises warrant outside military intervention. Most religious faiths have a universalistic streak to them, *i.e.*, that they incorporate some notion of common humanity, with concomitant calls to assist those in need, not just their fellow citizens or fellow adherents. In many cases, this leads religious leaders to an expansive concept of just cause in humanitarian crises. My own suggestion would be that they pay comparable attention to pragmatic, prudential ethical principles as well. This is what the just war *jus ad bellum* does in its totality. Taking into account both the principles of charity and of prudence would yield a fuller ethical analysis and would enable religious leaders to speak more clearly and relevantly to statesmen, who inhabit the world of prudence and pragmatism. Just as I argue that political and military leaders should

---

15 *Supra* note 11.

be at least conversant with the language of ethics, so too should religious leaders understand and be able to converse in the language of strategy.

There is another, perverse side to how religious leaders sometimes address issues of humanitarian interventions. There are those occasions in which some religious leaders are more likely to argue in favor of humanitarian interventions abroad when it is members of their faith who are suffering in other countries than when it is people of other or no particular faith. While the instinct to "take care of your own" is understandable, it is nonetheless difficult to reconcile with religious notions of common humanity or that all men and women are children of God.

Thus, there is, in conclusion and in my judgment, much reflection and creative thinking to be done by religious leaders on the question of when and how to intervene in humanitarian crises.

CHAPTER 7

RELIGION, LAW AND THE ROLE OF FORCE: OPERATIONAL ASPECTS

*General Andrew J. Goodpaster**

My interest in the role of force in conflict resolution extends back over many years, and was greatly heightened by the genocide in Bosnia during the past decade. In 1996 I participated in the work of the Carnegie Commission on preventing deadly violence, and offered my views in particular under the title, "When Diplomacy Is Not Enough." I intend here to comment on the points I made in my outline for this seminar, and to add a few further observations that are drawn from the seminar's discussion thus far.

To begin the consideration of the issues involved, we should think of using force in conflict resolution, I believe, where the problem is deemed serious enough to require action, and where it cannot be dealt with adequately by other means. Drawing from Clausewitz—that war is the continuation of policy by other means—it is helpful to set the role of military force in conflict resolution in the broader context of higher goals to be served, especially those of a humanitarian nature, in response to the policy decisions of our country's top leadership, acting on behalf of our people and their humanitarian interests and values. The conflicts to be resolved are, of course, of many differing kinds, extending from those in Haiti and Kuwait to those in Bosnia and Kosovo, interstate and intrastate alike. The efforts at conflict resolution have in common, however, a humanitarian purpose and content, and a defining goal of bringing deadly conflict to an end. But "resolution" broadly conceived goes much further. If it is to prove enduring, it must deal with the roots, sources and driving forces underlying the particular conflict concerned, and with the building of social and political institutions to provide justice, law and order, and human security.

It is in that wider context that military force may be brought in to serve. To that end, careful consideration of an approach and a framework

* The Eisenhower World Affairs Institute.

for the analysis, understanding and decisions that such a military role involves seems certain to be of value.

The approach suggested begins by identifying diplomacy, deterrence and defense as principal instruments or tools of influence and power for international action, to head off conflict or bring it to an end if it nevertheless occurs, *i.e.*, for "conflict resolution."

- "Diplomacy" is clearly the action that to the greatest possible extent is to be preferred. Such diplomacy includes a vast and valuable network of treaties, norms, international institutions, ongoing bilateral and multilateral agreements, negotiations, and like initiatives aimed at preventing violence, ameliorating conflict, resolving disputes and safeguarding human security.
- "Deterrence" comes through manifesting the will and capabilities, especially military (though the threat of economic sanctions can also be of value), to punish aggression or oppressions, and deny the fruits of violence and conflict to the aggressor or the perpetrator. The preferred result of deterrence is dissuasion—influencing a potential source of violence—government leaders or armed dissidents—*not* to resort to force, to escalate a conflict, or to oppose efforts to bring violence under control.
- "Defense" refers to all forms of military action, actually employing military force in support of conflict resolution. The commitment of military forces may range from imposing a cease-fire, as in Bosnia, or safeguarding civilian populations, collecting weapons, seizing and securing caches of arms, clearing mined areas, protecting lawful, established government, conducting combat operations as in Kosovo, to engaging in many forms of military action. Wise use of the defense instrument will look to the end-conditions that are to be sought and hopefully attained, from which clear military missions may be derived.

Though identified separately, these three are closely related in actuality, as the approach and framework suggested herein will indicate. The approach is simply to exercise and rely upon diplomacy first and foremost—diplomacy as a process well-grounded in international law—backed by deterrence and defense, all in support of U.S. interests and values—security, economic, humanitarian and environmental in particular. These stand in high importance to the well-being of America's people, including the deeply held sense of moral obligation that Americans bring to such issues.

But if diplomacy alone proves not to be enough, and deterrence should fail, then to be considered is the actual exercise of military force. Reaching an adequate degree of consensus in government and in the public as to which conflicts require and justify the use of force, and what kinds of force—especially the commitment of the U.S. military—becomes one of government's highest responsibilities. Differing views are surely to be expected and will need to be resolved. After the Vietnam experience, many will wish to reserve military commitment to the support only of interests of very high priority. Many have sounded notes of caution and restraint in this regard. Having worked closely with Dwight Eisenhower for many years, I can draw upon some of his views, first of all, "Be slow to pick up the sword." From him and others came the advice to reject a policy of "brushfire wars," arcane ideas of limited war, gunboat diplomacy, or service as a world policemen, a new era hegemony or a modern Rome, etc. Experience tells us, however, that when confronted by scenes of horror, such as pictured in the vicious, deep-rooted ethnic violence in the Balkans, the urge within the United States to "do something" will be very strong—acting alone if necessary but preferably in concert with other leading world democracies. Public support in such a case must, we know, be carefully assessed, and if called upon, be carefully maintained. And action by the government can and should be paralleled by efforts from the American society at large, including most notably initiatives of nongovernmental organizations devoted to such purposes.

Against this background and approach to the challenge, it is possible to outline a framework for careful consideration of the major issues involved in military intervention. We can set aside a question as to use of our military force in the case of actual attack or a threat of direct attack on the United States or its allies. In that case the issues are very much black and white. In humanitarian intervention, however, where the issues are shades of gray, many interests and values have to be balanced against each other. That, of course, is one of the highest duties of statesmen and most demanding tasks of the major institutions of government.

One key question is the consideration in depth of the desirability and the feasibility of undertaking such interventions, each of them presenting many unique features, taking into account all the aspects including costs and likelihood of success in furtherance of the totality of U.S. interests and values, broadly conceived, viewed and weighed as a whole by the responsible governmental authorities. The assessment can vary widely, depending on how far the mission is to reach. We have learned the great added difficulties, beyond efforts at cease-fires, that come with attempts at nation-building, or restoration of failed states. And to paraphrase Clausewitz again, we must seek to understand the nature of the conflict that the intervention is to deal with. Examples abound of numerous failures and occasional successes in that regard. Such failures include the ill-conceived Bay of Pigs undertaking and the failure to understand the North Vietnamese readiness to pay the price required for victory in

Vietnam. In contrast stand the successful recovery of Kuwait and the protection of Saudi Arabia in the Gulf War.

It is especially important to avoid mirror imaging, in particular because many nations are ruled by leaders of governments not "of the people, by the people, or for the people," but as police states or autocracies not motivated by the well-being of their nation's people. National pride, ambition and ego weigh heavily—the ambition, and pride, and ego of the leaders and their followers, including religious leaders of theocracies in important instances. There can be a driving urge simply to dominate. It is necessary to understand the source of the conflict, the motivations involved, the sources of power, and the possible avenues to end the conflict.

For us of the military, clarity of purpose and of mission are essential. A key question is always what end-state is really the goal? Is it an end to violence, stable peace, rule of law, and the prerequisites for economic and social development and justice? What costs will be involved, and what nature and scale of resources will need to be provided? What losses are to be expected and to be borne, for varying mission levels? What will our people be willing to support if the going becomes difficult—or if success is slow or uncertain of attainment? Is it to be a "no-U.S. casualties" operation? How is the intervention to be legitimized within the United States and internationally? Will it be sanctioned by the UN? Will it be viewed as *jus ad bello*? What support by the U.S. public and Congress may be counted on? The issues are profound; in Vietnam, with 50,000 American lives lost by the government's intervention, the Congress buckled and abandoned the U.S. ally. And can media pressures be borne—perhaps the principal question?

Next to be considered is who will conduct the operation. The United Nations, which offers legitimization but often lacks the necessary resources, support and international backing, has very limited capabilities, essentially limited to peacekeeping with the two contending sides in agreement. For peacemaking, enforcing a cease-fire, providing human security against violence, and a state of law and order, permitting peaceful development, in the terms suggested earlier, more powerful forces are required, together with the security institutions such as NATO or organized "coalitions of the willing and able" to furnish overall direction and guidance.

Few of the world's regional organizations are capable of this role, although it has been proposed by some that a standing force to act regionally be maintained in the UN, noting that regional means of responding can oftentimes be more effective than intervention from the outside, and from greater distance.

Finally, very briefly, there are challenging military operational requirements that must be attended to. First, there must be adequate and appropriate forces of a size and composition to provide the kind of capabilities needed to deal with a particular problem—and it is necessary to deal with very particular, very distinctive problems. Next come the command and control arrangements, clear channels that have to be constructed so as to provide for the necessary authority and responsibility within the framework of higher political direction. A system of arrangements to furnish a flow of intelligence of the quality, detail and timeliness needed, while protecting sensitive national sources and methods, constitutes the next prerequisite, without which military operations will be blind. And logistics are crucial. Such support includes necessary airlift, sealift and service support troops. Detailed information about local infrastructure, including water, fuel and power supplies and transportation systems, ports and airfields, along with health and other conditions that may affect operations, must be included in operational planning. As a strategic planner at the very close of World War II, I well recall the dictum of some of my logistics associates and colleagues: strategy proposes, logistics disposes.

Throughout all of this, there has to be training that prepares for and responds to the task at hand. The troops oftentimes have to be reoriented to a different kind of a mission, quite different from their normal duties. And, finally, it is not too much to say, regarding these operational requirements, if war is too important to be entrusted to generals, it is too difficult to be entrusted to amateurs.

From the foregoing, in brief summary conclusion: The role of force in conflict resolution can best be considered in the total context of such resolution efforts, extending from activities to head off such conflict to military intervention, motivated by humanitarian considerations in particular, and aimed at the building of an enduring post-hostilities civil structure based on justice, law and order. The possible call for such intervention poses a challenge that needs to be recognized in advance, thought through carefully at both high policy and operational levels, and prepared for as we look to the future.

PART II

RELIGION, LAW AND THE ROLE OF FORCE IN CONFLICT RESOLUTION

INTRODUCTION

At first glance, this title may seem an oxymoron, in that "conflict resolution" implies the agreement by all parties that peace is preferable to war, and that force should be abjured. However, this cannot always be. As noted earlier, humans frequently behave inhumanly to other humans: enslaving them, torturing them or mutilating them, driving them from their homes and their homeland and killing them by the thousands, whether in the ovens of Auschwitz or in the churches of Rwanda. And they do so despite earnest efforts at conciliating warring groups and at alleviating the poverty and lessening the inequalities which may incite violence, at helping to establish viable and acceptable political institutions and at trying to establish the rule of law. In short, there may be circumstances when the causes of conflict can be dealt with only by requiring the parties to that conflict to change their behavior—with force as a necessary means to this end.

There are occasions when that holds true among states; thus, the behavior of the Serbians vis-à-vis Bosnia in 1994–95 was widely viewed as justifying a forceful response, which was ultimately made. However, the majority of such actions, like those taken by the Arabized leaders of Northern Sudan against the largely black and non-Muslim peoples in the South, or the horrendous slaughter of Tutsis by Hutus in Rwanda, take place within states. And this poses several significant problems in authorizing the use of force:

- One is that while the three Abrahamic faith traditions may all condemn such violations of human rights, they do not have a common position on using force to stop them.

- Another is that the definition of rights varies among religions and with cultures, so that it is sometimes difficult to agree on transgressions that might justify intervention and even harder to agree on the basis for the "just peace" which armed humanitarian intervention (AHI) is to guarantee.
- A third is that there is no basis for AHI in international law unless the violence it is designed to stop can be classified as a threat to international peace and security and many legal objections to it because it violates state sovereignty.
- A fourth is that AHI is a difficult and demanding task, whose assumption few states welcome.

Our purpose here is to ascertain when, how and under what circumstances such use of force is warranted, *i.e.*, when transcendent ends justify unpalatable means. More specifically, we are interested in the role that religion can—and should—play in motivating and guiding the employment of force in the service of peace, both directly (through influencing decisions by officers and officials) and indirectly, by contributing to the framing of international law. Here we will both put forward some thoughts on those topics and look at one instance where an attempt was made to put theory into practice, in the former Yugoslavia.

RELIGION, LAW AND FORCE IN THEORY

Earlier in this book Professor Donald Shriver wrote "An Ethic of Humanitarian Intervention," in which he first reviewed the violations of human rights which warranted intervention, and then proceeded to state the principles that should govern decisions to intervene. As Professor Shriver made clear, these principles stem from the Christian teachings on "just war," which are adhered to by many (though not all) of the Christian churches. And he concluded, borrowing from the Resolution passed by the General Assembly of the Presbyterian Church of the United States in 1998, that stopping conflict is not enough: "just peace thinking must be taken as a holistic concern."[1]

In this part of the book, Professor David Little, starting from another base, comes to much the same conclusion. He notes that Hugo Grotius, in his seminal work, *Prolegomena to the Law of War and Peace*, argued that "War ought not be undertaken save for the enforcement of rights."[2] Moreover, not only Grotius but others have based this conclusion not just on the principles of their religion but on the notion that human rights

[1] Shriver, Donald. "Án Ethic of Humanitarian Intervention: A Post-September 11 Perspective."

[2] Grotius, Prolegomena, p, 18, quoted in David Little's paper, "Humanitarian Intervention: A Theoretical Approach."

were guaranteed by "natural" law.[3] And, to go a step further, many of these rights are protected by international law, beginning with the Geneva Convention of 1864 and including provisions found in the Charter of the United Nations. Nor has that body hesitated to condemn their violation and on occasion to impose sanctions on the violators.

The difficulty arises when this is not enough, when "crimes against humanity" continue, reaching a level where they can be characterized as "ethnic cleansing" or even as "genocide." In circumstances where the government is either unable or unwilling to put a stop to such behavior, the sole effective remedy may be the application of force by outsiders.

As Professor Little points out, the physician may have trouble applying that remedy. Armed intervention, even for humanitarian purposes, runs contrary to the Charter of the United Nations, with its emphasis upon sovereignty and the rights of states. It is a difficult and demanding task, particularly if it seeks to achieve a "just peace" rather than merely the imposition of order. As General Goodpaster noted earlier, it raises many questions about the size and the composition of the intervening forces, about the cost of the operation and, above all, about the command and control of the units engaged. All these tend to reinforce the reluctance of nations to sponsor, or even to contribute to, interventionary forces.

While acknowledging this, Professor Little believes that both natural law and morality are on the side of armed humanitarian intervention, a belief which he buttresses by an analysis of the case for intervention in Kosovo, using the critera of "just war" theory. Little's assessment, which is detailed in his chapter, reflects the very real difficulty of reaching agreement on the necessity for, and the nature of AHI; as one student of the topic remarked, "What may seem to you [interveners] like a fairy wand may look to the man on the ground like a baseball bat." Moreover, it is hard to see how consensus can be achieved, since some political leaders will oppose intervention anywhere for fear it will be practiced against them, some prelates from essentially ethnic churches may support their fellow nationals rather than the moral precepts which that religion embodies, and some governments may simply shy away from the difficult and costly task of AHI, especially where this leads directly to the even more difficult and costly task of nation-building. At the very least, we will have to tolerate many—and ugly—violations of human rights if we are to retain the possibility of using force against the perpetrators of still more beastly crimes.

Moreover, we may well, for the reasons listed above, have to find a way to link AHI to national (and organizational) interests. Few governments are so moved by compassion that that sentiment alone will induce them to undertake military operations; in fact, a prominent school of political

3 Nardin, "The Moral Basis of Humanitarian Intervention."

philosophy argues that "realism" not only should but must determine national security policy. Without denying the importance of upholding the interests of the state, we argue that these must include the promotion of the "common morality"—the creation and support of effective and just institutions that can protect the innocent against violence.[4] How this is to be done is a subject for debate; that it is to be done should not be.

RELIGION, LAW AND FORCE IN PRACTICE

As we would all agree, AHI is not an end in itself but a means to an end: the creation (or recreation) of a "just order." And as I think we would also agree, success in this endeavor depends in part on the nature of the society with which we must work, in part on our understanding of the situation and in part on our choice of instruments.

Professor Mojzes, in his chapter "Religion and Armed Humanitarian Intervention in the Former Yugoslavia," argues that the Western powers made a number of mistakes in their assessment of the situation in Yugoslavia-and consequently in their selection of instruments. Among other things:

- They underestimated the importance of symbols and historical myths, which led to the Serbian fixation on retaining dominance over Kosovo, "The Field of Blackbirds;" the site of their defeat by the Turks in 1389.
- They did not fully appreciate that religion, because of its identity with particular ethnic groups, might be an obstacle to peace and reconciliation rather than an asset; although some religious leaders called for peace, others blessed the troops marching off to war.
- They largely ignored the history of prior conflicts in Yugoslavia, which pitted one ethnic group against another and led to bitterness and hatred that is both strong and persistent.
- Perhaps in consequence, they expected that the Dayton Agreement for the creation of a tri-partite Bosnia would lead both to a functioning multi-ethnic government and the repatriation and resettlement of refugees, regardless of ethnicity. And they anticipated a similar adjustment between Albanian and Serbian Kosovars, when in fact the former, turning the tables, have been driving out the few Serbs who stayed behind after NATO forces entered the territory.

The prospect of having to cope with such problems is what has discouraged countries from undertaking AHI; the military operation, however difficult, is far less so than reconstruction. For one thing, it leaves

---

4 Nardin, *loc. cit.* p. 21.

the occupiers with a kind of Hobson's choice: nurturing elected governments which are uncooperative or forcefully restructuring them, to the detriment of teachings about democracy. For another, it may even mean occupying the territory for a generation or leaving the occupants free to make war on each other again. For a third, it can raise once more the issue of self-determination, with Albanians, for example, seeking to unite all those of the same blood in Kosovo, in Macedonia and in Albania proper. A statesman once wrote, "If Austria did not exist, it would be necessary to invent it." Perhaps the same message should have been sent to those who started the break-up of Yugoslavia in 1991.

All this is distressing but it should not preclude efforts to stop massive violations of human rights. What it does is suggest that those efforts start earlier and include a range of political, economic and military measures aimed at discouraging strife before it reaches the level at which AHI may be necessary. These we will put forward for your consideration after we have all reviewed the chapters by Professors Little and Mojzes.

CHAPTER 8

HUMANITARIAN INTERVENTION: A THEORETICAL APPROACH

*Dr. David Little**

INTRODUCTION

As James Johnson makes clear in the opening pages of his chapter in this volume, the subject of armed humanitarian intervention (AHI) poses a fundamental challenge to the existing international order. Judge Richard Goldstone's opinion, which Johnson cites, that the military campaign in Kosovo carried out by the North Atlantic Treaty Organization between March 24 and June 10 1999, constituted a permissible violation of the United Nations Charter, succinctly summarizes that challenge. Forceful intervention in the internal affairs of a sovereign state without Security Council authorization, whether for humanitarian or any other reasons, is clearly outlawed by the charter. As a matter of fact, in its present form, the charter does not appear to recognize repression and mistreatment inside a state as a legitimate reason for armed intervention at all. Yet, in the light of the Kosovo experience, Goldstone is not alone in boldly "questioning the appropriateness and the applicability" of this understanding of the charter. Indeed, the challenge he has articulated has inspired a deep and pervasive reconsideration of the existing norms of international life.

Religious bodies the world around are fitting participants in this process of reconsideration. During and after the operation in Kosovo, religious representatives publicly defended or condemned the effort, and they can be expected to continue commenting on the subject. Religions characteristically give attention to reasons for supporting or renouncing force, and the question of humanitarian intervention simply intensifies their concern, since protecting and assisting the vulnerable and mistreated has especially strong resonance in most religious traditions.

---

* Professor of Religious Studies and Director, Center for the Study of Values in Public Life, Harvard Divinity School.

Insofar as religious communities do become involved in this important process of reconsideration, the starting point needs to be the existing order and its adequacy or inadequacy. That is, the United Nations system, including the charter, and its current interpretation, sets the proper context for religious reflection. The reason is that the UN system defines the existing norms for the international use of force, and these norms must either be accepted or changed. Furthermore, the system is itself the product of continuing international and intercultural dialogue and interaction, a process that needs to be extended and deepened.

As one contribution to the religious reconsideration of the norms of international life, particularly as they bear on humanitarian intervention, I shall characterize and elaborate on the contribution of the liberal Reformed wing of the Christian tradition. I have chosen that part of the Christian tradition for two reasons:

- The first is that it has, as Donald Shriver's earlier chapter indicates, gone further than others, whether Christian or non-Christian, in endorsing the concept of AHI and in defining the features which should justify its application and shape its nature;
- The second is that the lineage of thought from those of this persuasion has had, and continues to have, important (if not altogether conclusive) things to say about our subject.

I shall proceed by representing the thought of an important 17th-century member of the tradition, Hugo Grotius (1583–1645). He is chosen for the profundity of his ideas about religion, morality, and force, as well as for the fact that his thought influenced the present international order in a decisive way. In addition, Grotius's ideas contain some interesting suggestions concerning our current perplexities over humanitarian intervention and related subjects.

At the heart of Grotius's thinking, and the key to what he regarded as the foundation of intercultural and international harmony and peace, is a belief in a common morality implicitly shared by all the world, and taken as relatively independent of particular religions and cultures. The belief in a common moral law of humanity was controversial in Grotius's time and it has remained so to the present. At the same time, the idea has made headway, for example, as the basis of the system of international human rights and humanitarian law, adopted after World War II. These developments are thoroughly consonant with Grotius's convictions and expectations.

Grotius was a Dutch public official and legal scholar, whose most famous work was *The Law of War and Peace*, published in 1625. His career and thought were deeply affected by religion. Reared in the Dutch Reformed tradition, he came to side with the Remonstrants, a liberal group opposed to orthodox Calvinism in a conflict of intense hostility and sometimes violence. Wherever Grotius looked, he saw the bitter fruit of religiously tinged combat, most vividly in the Thirty Years War that was devastating Europe at the time he wrote his book on war and peace. At the beginning of that book he records his revulsion at such a specter, remarking that throughout the Christian world there could be observed "a lack of restraint in relation to war, such as even barbarous races should be ashamed of. . . ." He found, he said, "that men rush to arms for slight causes, or no cause at all, and that when arms have once been taken up there is no longer any respect for law, divine or human; it is as if, in accordance with a general decree, frenzy had been openly let loose for the committing of all crimes."[1]

PRINCIPLES OF RESTRAINT

Underlying Grotius's proposals for rectifying the frenzy and brutality of war he witnessed all around him was a conviction that religion and force must be separated. For Grotius, there are both religious and nonreligious grounds for such a conviction. "It is plain," he wrote, "that no force should be used with nations to promote [Christianity's] acceptance," because Christian truth cannot be accepted "without the secret assistance of God."[2] If people do not believe at once, that is the result of "reasons that are generally unknown to us, and [that are] therefore not punishable by human judgments."[3] There is, he says, "another reason of no less weight, which is that Christ, being the author of a new law, will have no one brought to embrace his doctrine by fear of human punishments."

Beyond that, Grotius believed that human beings are capable of coming to certain common practical conclusions independent of special religious enlightenment or inspiration, because they share a moral capacity made up of "certain fundamental conceptions that are beyond question, so that no one can deny them without doing violence to [one]self." On Grotius's account, there is ready recognition that without good reason for doing so, such as protection against arbitrary injury or punishment for mistreatment, human beings may not be killed, or subjected to intense pain, disablement, or confinement, or to other injurious consequences of the application of force.

Consequently, Grotius asserts, in a famous statement, that the "natural" moral limits on the use of force "would have a degree of validity even if we should concede . . . that there is no God, or that the affairs of men are of no concern to him."[4] By explicitly disconnecting the moral

1 HUGO GROTIUS, PROLEGOMENA TO THE LAW OF WAR AND PEACE 21 (Francis W. Kelsey trans., 1957).

2 HUGO GROTIUS, THE RIGHTS OF WAR AND PEACE 253–54 (A.C. Campbell, trans., 1979).

3 *Id.*

4 GROTIUS, *supra* note 1, at 10.

basis of his approach from religion, Grotius was able by implication to transcend the very religious conflicts that were causing so much trouble during his lifetime. He could thereby broaden the appeal of his effort to uncover a common law of humanity according to which to mitigate the chaos of war taking place all around him.

It is against this background that Grotius developed his version of just war theory, a version that came to exert important influence on the modern laws of war. As was conventional, he drew a distinction between the justice of going to war (*jus ad bellum*) and the just conduct of war (*jus in bello*).

In order to satisfy the first category, a proposed use of force must meet several standards. It must be authorized by *legitimate authority*, which, for Grotius, should be understood more in secular than ecclesiastical terms, and, ideally, should be constituted by a confederation of states. It must serve a *just cause*, identified by Grotius in terms of the three traditional "good reasons" for using force: self-defense, protection of property (including the recovery of stolen assets), and the correction of wrongdoing. It should be undertaken with a *peaceful intention*, and only as a *last resort* (namely, after all peaceful means of resolution have been exhausted). It should conform to the standard of *general proportionality*, which means that the cause for war, even if just, must be grave or weighty enough to risk life and national treasure, and the overall benefits of using force must outweigh the costs. There must be a *reasonable hope of success*, so as to avoid turning combat into a senseless and wasteful exercise in futility. Lastly, there needs to be *formal declaration of war*, including a list of charges, so as to insure full accountability.

As to the just conduct of war, Grotius mentions three items: *Military proportionality*, as distinct from "general proportionality," means that weapons and tactics must be morally and materially efficient in the pursuit of military objectives. In regard to the *treatment of prisoners*, and the *protection of noncombatants*, Grotius makes a distinctive contribution to the just war tradition. He sharply criticizes prevailing customs according to which prisoners might permissibly be executed and women and children abused, enslaved or killed, arguing that such treatment is contrary to the dictates of "humanity." According to those dictates, he says, "the greatest precaution should be used against involving the innocent in danger. . . ."[5]

In the light of Grotius's just war teaching, the significance of his basic theory of war stands out: "War ought not be undertaken except for the enforcement of rights."[6] In a word, force has no other purpose than the protection of the rights of all human beings not to be killed, confined,

---

5 GROTIUS, *supra* note 2, at 361.

6 GROTIUS, *supra* note 1, at 18.

injured or dispossessed, and every exercise of force must finally be judged in keeping with that standard. Accordingly, Grotius is correctly thought of as the "true ancestor of all modern codes which have . . . rights at their centre,"[7] and he should be included "among the founding forefathers of our modern doctrine of human rights."[8]

Grotius meant what he said about the enforcement of rights as the primary purpose of war. While he honors the right of self-defense, he does not restrict the use of force to that. He goes out of his way to emphasize the importance of another of the traditional just causes for using force, the correction of wrongdoing—or, the curtailment, in his words, of "such treatment as no one is warranted in inflicting." In a little-known passage, Grotius leaves no doubt about his views in this respect:

> If, however, the wrong is obvious, in case [a leader] should inflict upon his subjects such treatment as no one is warranted in inflicting, the exercise of the right [to intervene] vested in human society is not precluded. . . . If, further, it should be granted that even in extreme need subjects cannot justifiably take up arms . . . , nevertheless it will not follow that others may not take up arms on their behalf. . . . Hence, . . . I may make war upon one who is not one of my people but oppresses his own, as we said when dealing with the infliction of punishment, a procedure which is often connected with the protection of innocent persons. We know, it is true, from both ancient and modern history that the desire for what is another's seeks such pretexts as this for its own ends; but a right does not at once cease to exist in case it is to some extent abused by evil men.[9]

Many of Grotius's ideas contained in the *Law of War and Peace* eventually found their way into the modern laws of war, even if, as they stand, those laws do not represent the full range of Grotius's views, particularly in regard to armed humanitarian intervention. The Hague Regulations of 1899 and 1907 and the United Nations Charter, as well as the 1949 Geneva Conventions on the protection of the vicitms of war, and the Additional Protocols of 1977, codify and expand on Grotius's proposals. For example, article 51 of the UN Charter, which acknowledges the inherent right of national self-defense, enshrines one of the just causes for war which Grotius emphasized. Chapter VII of the charter identifies the Security Council as the ultimate legitimate authority for determining the use of force among states, embodying the collective character of international

---

7 Richard Tuck, Natural Rights Theories: Their Origins and Development 66 (1981).

8 Geoffrey Best, War and Law Since 1945 28 (1994).

9 Hugo Grotius, Law of War and Peace 584 (Francis W. Kelsey trans., 1925).

authority that Grotius recommended. Articles 41 and 42 express the just war standard of last resort, according to which force may be used only after less violent measures have been tried. Grotius also made a good deal of these provisions.

The Geneva Conventions and the Additional Protocols provide guidance for the conduct of war in ways that reflect both Grotius's *in bello* principles and his distinctive emphasis on the connection between force and rights. Article 40 of the First Protocol requires that military operations respect the distinction between "the civilian population and combatants and between civilian objects and military objectives." Article 50.5(b) provides that attacks causing indirect and unintentional injury to civilians "must not be excessive in relation to the concrete and direct military advantage anticipated." The Third Geneva Convention provides elaborate protection for the humane treatment of prisoners of war, recalling Grotius's special concern with that subject. Article 3, common to all of the Geneva Conventions, guarantees absolute protection against various forms of brutal treatment to all "persons taking no part in the hostilities, including members of the armed forces who have laid down their arms and those placed *hors de combat*. . . ."

ARMED HUMANITARIAN INTERVENTION AND THE CHALLENGE TO INTERNATIONAL ORDER

The debate over armed humanitarian intervention, which we mentioned at the beginning, and which is illustrated by the NATO military intervention into sovereign Yugoslavian territory without UN authorization, can be seen as the result of unresolved tensions within the just war tradition, particularly as it is inherited from Hugo Grotius. While the UN Charter was, as we saw, heavily influenced by that tradition, the charter nevertheless embodied the tradition in a very one-sided way. Such things as advancing human rights and promoting justice are emphasized throughout the charter, but they are strictly isolated from the grounds for using force. As Louis Henkin has pointed out, the charter has a "status quo bias." It is exclusively disposed to protect the sovereignty of states against forceful interference of any sort. Self-defense, allowed by article 51, is consistent with that bias, as is the pervasive use of the phrase, "international peace and security." As the charter stands, "peace [is] more important than progress and more important than justice."[10]

At the same time, such a bias is by no means consistent with Grotius's theory. The idea that "war ought not be undertaken except for the enforcement of rights" is rather different from the prescription that better fits the charter: "war ought not be undertaken except for the enforcement of state

---

[10] Louis Henkin, et al., Right versus Might: International Law and the Use of Force 38 (2d ed. 1991).

sovereignty." Moreover, Grotius's idea that the enforcement of rights might entail a wholehearted commitment to humanitarian intervention seems to move beyond the present compass of the charter, and challenges us, as Judge Goldstone put it, to question "the appropriateness and the applicability" of the charter in its existing form.

No less a figure that the Secretary General of the United Nations, Kofi Annan, has echoed—albeit unwittingly—Grotius's concern about the connection between force and rights and the permissibility of armed humanitarian intervention. In a portentous speech, delivered in 1998,[11] Annan publicly and expressly criticized what he calls "old orthodoxy," which dominates current understanding of the United Nations Charter. In the name of protecting state sovereignty and international stability, the old orthodoxy, says Annan, would counsel inaction "so long as a conflict rages within the borders of a single state. . . ." A conflict may be left "to 'burn itself out,' . . . and [even] to escalate, regardless of human consequences, at least until the point when its effects . . . spill over into neighboring states, so that it becomes . . . 'a threat to international peace and security.'"

The Secretary General knows whereof he speaks. In the name of the old orthodoxy, the UN General Assembly explicitly refused to endorse such arguably urgent humanitarian efforts as the Indian intervention in East Pakistan in 1971, which brought an end to the bloody civil war there, or the intervention by Vietnam in Cambodia in 1978, which halted the genocidal rule of Pol Pot and the Khmer Ruge, or Tanzania's intervention in Uganda in 1979, undertaken for the purpose of overthrowing the brutal regime of Idi Amin. UN resistance occurred because the interventions were unilateral and unauthorized. But, says Annan, history has subsequently vindicated those actions. "Few would now deny that in those cases intervention was a lesser evil than allowing massacre and extreme oppression to continue."[12]

For Annan, these examples of UN failure are deeply disturbing. "The United Nations Charter, after all, was issued," he says, "in the name of 'peoples,' not [of] governments. . . . Its aim is not only to preserve international peace—vitally important though that is—but also 'to reaffirm faith in fundamental human rights and, in the dignity and worth of the human person.' . . . It was never meant as a license for governments to trample on human rights and human dignity. . . ."[13]

Drawing some very practical conclusions in respect to Kosovo, which at the time of Annan's speech was already threatening to explode, the Secretary General proceeded to endorse "the clear determination expressed by NATO . . . to prevent further escalation of the fighting [in Kosovo],"

---

11 Secretary-General Kofi Annan, Ditchley Lecture 2 (June 26, 1998).

12 *Id.* at 5.

13 *Id.* at 2.

and to "encourage all steps that may deter the further use of ethnically driven repression and the resort to force in Kosovo." He clearly implies that the use of force will have to be considered as part of that policy.[14]

It must be said that while the Secretary General encourages both individual states and regional organizations to consider undertaking armed humanitarian intervention in extreme circumstances, he assumes that that should be done only with the sanction of the United Nations. All such operations, he says, will "need to have the authority of the Security Council behind them, expressed in an authorizing resolution."[15] Mr. Annan clearly believes that the charter can and should be reinterpreted to make room for armed humanitarian intervention. However, he does not reflect on what is to be done when, as in the case of Kosovo—a year after his ground-breaking speech was delivered, the imperative of humanitarian intervention directly conflicts with the demand for Security Council authorization.

ARMED HUMANITARIAN INTERVENTION AND THE ROLE OF FORCE

The decision to engage in AHI poses at least as many problems as does the question of authorization. For one thing, that decision necessarily involves national interests. As history has shown, states may well fail to act in face of the bloodiest of repressions because they do not believe intervention will serve their interests. Indeed, they may consider intervention by anyone to be contrary to their interests, as did Russia in the case of Bosnia and as did China in the case of Cambodia. However such a response is assessed, it is a fact of life, and it may be very difficult to overcome.

Unless a given state possesses the disposition and capacity to act on its own, it must try to mobilize a multilateral effort. This can have both political and military benefits. The broader the coalition, the less likely intervention will be seen to serve the narrow interests of a single state. Such a coalition may also help militarily, by providing bases, troops, aircraft and specialized technical capabilities that may exceed the capabilities of any one state.

But whatever the political or military benefits, coalition warfare is not an unmixed blessing. (Napoleon reputedly said, "Let me always fight against alliances.") As General Goodpaster pointed out earlier, and as the experience of the UN in Bosnia prior to the NATO takeover demonstrated, such operations frequently lack common objectives, to say nothing of unity of command, a cohesive military doctrine and a functioning logis-

---

[14] *Id.* at 5.

[15] *Id.* at 7.

tic system. All of these may have to be arranged hastily, with consequent delays, inefficiencies and failures.

Nor is this all. Different commanders have different views as to what constitutes "unacceptable losses" in both human and material terms. Sometimes this judgment is a personal one: thus, General George B. McClellan, Commanding General of the Union Army in 1862, held very different views about what constitutes "unacceptable losses" of men and material from his successor, General Ulysses S. Grant. Sometimes it is professional, as was true of German General Eric von Falkenhayn, when he accepted enormous losses in an effort to destroy the French army at Verdun in 1916. Sometimes it mirrors a political decision, as in the reluctance of U.S. leadership, prior to September 11, to tolerate any military casualties at all. In any event, imposing rigid limits on the kinds of risks that are acceptable and the nature of those operations that will be tolerated can seriously impede military effectiveness, as, some have argued, occurred in the Kosovo campaign.

ARMED HUMANITARIAN INTERVENTION IN KOSOVO

The just war tradition has never been particularly helpful in providing a method for resolving tensions or conflicts in the application of the eight or so standards according to which judgments about the justice of a particular use of force are to be made. Neither Grotius nor other formative just war thinkers seriously or successfully addressed this issue. But, as we know, that is exactly the problem we face in a case like Kosovo, and, as a matter of fact, the tensions and conflicts in applying the just war standards turn out to be even more perplexing in this case than we have indicated so far.

This was in part because, as Paul Mojzes has noted in his chapter, the situation was a tangled one. First of all, Kosovo had to some extent been "at war" since the activation in 1998 of the Kosovo Liberation Army, which carried out guerilla operations against both the Serbian Army and the Serbs living in Kosovo. Thus, Serbia could—and did—claim that it was simply restoring order. Second, this was the sixth in a series of upheavals which had, during the prior decade, led to wars in Slovenia, in Croatia and in Bosnia-Herzegovina, wars that resulted in the dismemberment of Yugoslavia and stiffened the Serbian resolve to keep control of Kosovo. Thirdly the emergence, during the long series of clashes between members of ethno-religious groups, of a belief that "might makes right" made it difficult to devise ways to resolve the conflict in Kosovo and even more difficult to establish a "just peace."

There is the obvious problem, already introduced, of how to reconcile the standards of *legitimate authority* and *just cause.* The legitimate authority for certifying all cross-border uses of force is the UN Security

Council, and yet, as we have mentioned, NATO undertook armed humanitarian intervention in Kosovo without ever soliciting or receiving Security Council authorization. The Security Council was simply ignored, because it was assumed (no doubt correctly) that Russia and China would veto military action in Kosovo. Nor was the possibility of intervention by a single state seriously considered, since the only conceivable candidate was an already very reluctant United States. At bottom, the intervention was defended in the name of one of the traditional just causes—the correction of wrongdoing, or, in Kofi Annan's terms, "to deter the further use of ethnically driven repression and the resort to violence by either side." But, unlike self-defense, the correction of wrongdoing has not until very recently been given any authoritative attention within the UN system.

It seems obvious that the new emphasis on humanitarian intervention and "the enforcement of rights" as a just cause for the international use of force has struck a deep common moral nerve, and for that reason has emerged as an irrepressible contemporary concern. However one may finally assess the intervention in Kosovo, there can be little doubt that real-world circumstances, such as the genocide in Rwanda, make it very hard to go on ignoring the urgency and importance of the correction of wrongdoing as a cause for using force. Grotius would have been surprised only by how long it has taken the world to appreciate the fact, since that cause is so essential to protecting the ideal of "humanity," as he understands it, and therefore to achieving international justice and peace.

It also seems clear that a way will have to be found to bring the UN system into line with this new imperative, even though it is by no means clear just how that will be done. Appealing as it is, the idea of generalizing a right of armed humanitarian intervention poses a severe threat to the national interests of many states around the world, as we have mentioned. The prospect of facing armed intervention aimed at "enforcing rights" inside "the domestic jurisdiction of any state" (in the words of art. 2(7) of the UN Charter), represents a revolution in international understanding that will hardly be welcome in many quarters. Moreover, continuing to permit or condone such action without UN authorization, as happened in Kosovo, will be regarded as especially offensive.

In addition to this perplexity, the Kosovo case raises other questions about the application of just war standards. The standard of *peaceful intention* poses the problem of the conditions of withdrawal of the Kosovo Force (KFOR). We are probably safe in assuming that none of the members of NATO wishes to remain in permanent possession of Kosovo but how shall we know when peace has been achieved and assured to a degree sufficient that the Kosovars and their Yugoslavian countrymen can be left to themselves? A Grotian response would dictate that a sufficiently just and stable peace had been attained when indigenous institutions are capable of "enforcing rights" on their own account, and are thus able to prevent the recurrence of the conditions that generated the call for armed humanitarian intervention in the first place. Consistent and reasonable as such an indication would be, applying it still involves two difficulties: one is deciding exactly when that point has been achieved, and the other is sustaining the perseverance of the members of KFOR toward such an objective.

Given the uncertainty of knowing whether the situation in Kosovo will ever achieve the desired degree of justice and stability, applying the standard of *a reasonable chance of success* there has always been somewhat problematical. Given the strong opposition to a merger of Kosovo with other territories inhabited predominately by Albanians—a prospect which has upset Macedonians as well as Serbians—a "greater Albania" seems an unlikely outcome. An independent Kosovo would seem to many to be simply a preliminary step toward this outcome. Conversely, a self-governing Kosovo could be reestablished as a part of Serbia but this would require both a degree of abnegation on the part of Serbia that may not be forthcoming and a degree of tolerance on the part of the Kosovars that may not emerge. Over time, we can hope that a rejuvenated Kosovo may be incorporated into a restructured European Union or administered by some form of United Nations mandate, but for the moment these are just dreams. Any realistic vision for the time being must involve the continuing participation of NATO.

The difficulty with the standard of *last resort* is raised by the Rambouillet Agreement that was arrived at prior to the NATO military action, and that served as a warrant for the intervention. The agreement had all the earmarks of a contrivance generated not by sincere and serious negotiations, but by an act of "coercive diplomacy" on the part of NATO.[16] Even if it is argued, as it might be, that the Milosovic government was not in any case "ready to deal," and therefore that efforts at peaceful settlement were already exhausted by the time the Rambouillet meeting took place,[17] the terms of ultimate settlement between the Serbian and Albanian communities in Kosovo were left very indeterminate, as was the ultimate connection between Kosovo and the Federal Republic of Yugoslavia.[18] In retrospect, more extensive efforts might have been made to arrive at an agreement, an observation which remains as valid for the future as for the past.

Finally, there are serious difficulties with applying the standard of *the protection of noncombatants.* There seems little doubt that the policy of high-

---

[16] Mark Danner, *Endgame in Kosovo: Ethnic Cleansing and American Amnesia, in* CONTENDING VOICES ON BALKAN INTERVENTIONS 68–69, 294 (William Joseph Buckley ed., 2000).

[17] *Id.* at 69.

[18] Henry Kissinger, *Kosovo and the Vicissitudes of American Foreign Policy, in* CONTENDING VOICES ON BALKAN INTERVENTIONS 294 (William Joseph Buckley ed., 2000).

altitude bombing undertaken in order to protect NATO pilots is, in just war terms, highly questionable. The principle of noncombatant immunity is not served by effectively shifting the burden of risk from combatants to noncombatants, as happened as a matter of consistent practice in the bombing of Serbia, and on occasion in the bombing of Kosovo. More importantly, there is the question whether NATO ground operations, though admittedly more difficult and more costly than aerial bombardment, might not have brought to an end more quickly the mass deportations which forced hundreds of thousands of Kosovars into Albania or Macedonia and disrupted the entire society. There are, of course, the familiar political arguments in favor of giving priority to the protection of allied forces. However, protection of combatants is not a convincing basis for compromising the standard of noncombatant protection. If armed humanitarian intervention is licitly to be undertaken in the future, greater provision will have to be made for the welfare of noncombatants.

CONCLUSION

We have, we hope, made three major points. One is that the just war tradition is at present alive and well, at least insofar as it provides crucial moral reference points for determining the justifiability of the international use of force. The second point is that as potent and persistent as the tradition is, it contains a number of inner tensions and conflicts making its application under present circumstances perplexing. One of those perplexities concerns the status of armed humanitarian intervention in the existing international order. On the one hand, there appears to be a compelling moral case for it, a case that has deep historical roots in the just war tradition, as we have shown. On the other hand, the prospect of admitting a general right to armed humanitarian intervention threatens strong national interests of states around the world, and thus will likely encounter extensive resistance. Moreover, there are other problems and difficulties in applying just-war standards to a concrete case, like the Kosovo intervention, as we have tried to demonstrate.

The third major point is directly connected to the first two. Both because of the potency and the perplexity of the just-war tradition, there is need for continuing and active reflection on and reconsideration of the tradition by religious communities. We have shown, I hope, the enormous influence of liberal Reformed Christian thinking on the tradition, in the person of Hugo Grotius. His fundamental proposal that there exists a shared moral law of humanity that makes possible international cooperation and peace constitutes a noble invitation to intercultural and inter religious dialogue.

CHAPTER 9

RELIGION AND ARMED HUMANITARIAN INTERVENTION IN THE FORMER YUGOSLAVIA

*Dr. Paul Mojzes**

INTRODUCTION

The previous chapters in this volume are largely didactic: that is, they prescribe codes of conduct on modes of action based on religious principles, on the laws of war and on military ethics. As such, they are also largely abstract; only David Little's chapter endeavors to apply his conclusions to a particular case[1] and even this is (of necessity) illustrative rather than evaluative. My paper has been designed by the editors, and written by the author, to do three things:

- To provide an overview of the situation in the former Yugoslavia in the 1990s;
- To evaluate Professor Little's suggestions and the actual practice of "armed humanitarian intervention" in the former Yugoslavia, with particular reference to the intervention in Kosovo in 1998;
- From this, to draw some inferences as to the ways in which "humanitarian intervention" might be made more effective.

THE INFLUENCE OF HISTORY

The tendency of European scholars is to provide so much historical overview or other prolegomena that it is unlikely that one will get to the contemporary issues. The propensity of American scholars is to neglect much of the past and deal largely with the current situation, at the risk of not being able to understand it well for want of detecting the determining influences from the past. I have lived most of my life in the United States but some of my European training is still evident. So, while I will,

---

* Rosemont College.

1 *See supra* Ch. 8.

indeed, concentrate on the subject at hand, I will review those past events without which it is hard to understand the context of the most recent wars.

Since I am actually beginning to write this chapter the day after the terrorist attack on the World Trade Center and the Pentagon, the reader will appreciate the fact that after some event or events, life will never be the same again for the affected people. The people in the Balkans experienced a large number of extremely tragic events over the period of their history which—without making any artificial comparison of tragedies—had at least as profound an impact on their psyche and their future as the tragic events of September 11, 2001, are likely to have on us.

Some of these events stemmed from centuries-old colonialism and militarism. Roman, Byzantine, Frankish, Slavic, Venetian, Hungarian, Austrian, Turkish, Napoleonic, German, Russian, and most recently "the international" (in reality NATO) forces have overrun the area and used military and other force to impose their will over the local population. This was in addition to local rulers who used no less violent means to establish their own rule over whatever territory they could control. Not only has the population of these areas experienced unthinkable barbarities in these cruel historic processes but they became accustomed to expect that *force*, mostly military force, determined the outcome of events. Much of the population of all nationalities of the former Yugoslavia are quite willing to fatalistically accept that "might makes right."

Moreover, the Great Schism of Eastern and Western Christianity cut right across the Balkans. Those nearer Constantinople became followers of Eastern Orthodoxy and those closer to Rome of Roman Catholicism. This introduced a religious component to the wars between the various feudal principalities of the area. This state of affairs continued with the Turkish conquest in the 14th and 15th centuries, which brought under Ottoman rule not only the remnants of the Byzantine Empire but the territories of Bulgaria, Romania, Bosnia, Serbia, Croatia and part of Hungary. It also introduced Islam to the Balkans and the area became a place of encounter of three great faiths. Most, though not every aspect of the encounter, was characterized by conflict, suspicion, distrust, and, from time to time, outbreaks of violent hostility. Thus, the territory of former Yugoslavia became the ground where the three great religions, Eastern Orthodoxy, Roman Catholicism, and Islam meet in a permanent clash, although there were also times of peaceful and tolerant interactions.

An ethno-religious symbiosis gradually formed. Macedonians, Serbians, and Montenegrins are Orthodox; Slovenes and Croats are Catholic. Muslims did not at first have a specific ethnic identification (except that all Turks were Muslims) but later the sizeable Muslim population of Bosnia and Herzegovina came to see itself with the encouragement of the Communist Party as a "Muslim" nationality and by 1994 they themselves adopted the term "Boshniac" for their nationality. Ethnic

Albanians living in the successor states of the former Yugoslavia are almost all Muslims. There are numerous reasons for this juxtaposition of religion and ethnicity, including the strong Hapsburg pressure on the population living in its empire to be Catholic, which put pressure on the Orthodox to convert or become Uniate and created among the Orthodox a sense of permanent threat by Catholicism—sometimes even overshadowing in their minds the Islamic threat.

Another significant result of Turkish rule was the replacement of secular leaders by religious ones. In the lands of the Ottoman Empire people were divided by religion (the *millet* system). The religious leader of each non-Muslim group became the responsible leader of the respective ethnic community and this certainly contributed to the above-mentioned symbiotic relationship between religion and nation. Thus, the religious and national communities are co-extensive, to the degree that even non-religious people of the ethnic group are regarded as latent members of the prevailing religion.

The disintegration of the Ottoman Empire, and the consequent shifts in the positions of the local communities, led to further turmoil. During the 20th century alone there were five major wars: the First Balkan War, 1912; the Second Balkan War, 1913; World War I, 1914–1918; World War II, 1941–1945; and the wars of the late 20th century. These latter were complex and exceedingly violent stages of disintegration of the federation we knew as Yugoslavia, cooked up mostly but not solely by domestic players after Tito's death. International interventions (political, diplomatic, and economic) sometimes tended toward resolution of the problems but at other times inflamed the conflict. One may simply say that there was both internal and external encouragement of the disintegration of Yugoslavia.

During the last two decades of the 20th century in Yugoslavia there were actually five (or perhaps six) distinct wars:

a. The low intensity wars in Kosovo and Croatia, mostly in the 1980s, which were outbursts of terrorism based on both ancient and more recent ethnic animosities and grievances.
b. The war in Slovenia (1991), a brief war of the Federal Government of Yugoslavia against the Republic of Slovenia due to the latter's secessionist moves.
c. The war in Croatia (1991–1995), when Serbs living in regions where they made up a sizeable portion of the population such as the Krajina and Eastern Slavonia, supported by the Yugoslav federal army and Serbian paramilitaries, fought to prevent the secession of Croatia, and having failed to do so, to secede from Croatia.
d. The war in Bosnia and Herzegovina (1992–1995), a war of the Yugoslav federal army, siding with Bosnian Serbs, to prevent

secession by the newly proclaimed independent country, which gradually transformed itself into a three-way civil war between Bosnian Serbs, Croats and Muslims (Boshniancs).[2]

And,

e. The war over Kosovo (1998), in which the "Kosovo Liberation Army" rebelled for the purpose of seceding from Serbia, gaining international sympathies and leading to an air war by NATO against rump Yugoslavia, resulting in a UN protectorate over Kosovo.
f. A sixth war, so far of low intensity, is taking place in Macedonia, pitting a group of ethnic Albanian terrorists, mostly from Kosovo, against the democratically elected government of Macedonia. After almost a year of conflict, beginning in February 2001, the two sides have agreed on an uneasy truce, monitored by an international force, which may or may not lead to a settlement of differences.

In brief, the peoples of the Balkan peninsula have been undergoing radical changes during the last century, changes which have caused enormous crises of identity. Collectively but even individually these people had been subjects of multinational empires, then citizens of burgeoning nation-states, then occupied by Axis Powers, then part of the socialist/communist block, then members of a national-communist independent state, and most recently citizens of ethnic successor states (some of them being exiled or occupied by one ethnic state, then becoming residents of another). They had experienced feudal and patriarchal social systems, then nascent capitalism, then fascism, then socialism-Titoism, and finally post-Communism. The post-Communist period is characterized by ambiguities but it appears to be a struggle between reverting to a tribal vs. aspiring toward a "European/democratic" model. Often times the identities were formed predominantly by deciding who the enemy is and then trying to differentiate oneself from that "other."

Helpful in understanding the clash of these cultures is the iceberg paradigm.[3] Most of the collisions take place under the surface as the more massive part of the iceberg is not visible and is wider and deeper than the visible part. On the surface icebergs seem to be co-existing, but underneath a lot of clashing and bumping takes place. The colonization of the Balkans by the great empires resulted in the meltdown of the visible part of local cultures, pushing below the surface a great deal of the self-identity. On the surface people are modern Europeans but under the surface

---

[2] For a relatively concise summary of the first four conflicts *see* PAUL MOJZES, YUGOSLAVIAN INFERNO: ETHNORELIGIOUS WARFARE IN THE BALKANS 87–124 (1994).

[3] The imagery comes from ERIC H. F. LAW, THE WOLF SHALL DWELL WITH THE LAMB TOGETHER (1993).

lurks a great deal of unresolved sense of being threatened by those who inhabit the same or adjacent space. Each group is trying to figure out what needs to be protected; what they can give up and what they must protect at all cost. In that process it is not determinative what is actually historical, but what the group selects to remember and emphasize, namely the mytho-historical perspective. Stuart Kaufman pointed out that the "symbolic policy" of identity utilizes myth, which is "a combination of truth, fancy, and more or less arguable opinions. . . . [W]hat matters politically is what people believe—that is, the mythology, not little-known historical truths."[4] Thus, in the post-Communist period as well as in earlier ones, people seek to gain security—which is a rational goal—by means of collective identities which are based on the appeal of emotion rather than on calculated group or individual interest. These emotions are directed and manipulated by political leaders who use the myths to mobilize people to action.[5]

RELIGION AND CONFLICT

Religion's Contribution to War

In a previous work I have characterized the role of religion as being "camouflaged."[6] People in the Balkans generally do not tend to display their religion overtly. Communist rule certainly had much to do with that as it had insisted that religion be a private matter and that if expressed it be done quite discretely. Religion seems to be implicit and collective, a pre-Enlightenment phenomenon. Religion is determined by one's ethnicity rather than by choice. Religious leadership practices exclusively a priestly form of religion (that applies even to Islam, which does not have a formal priesthood), by which is meant that the role of the leadership is to protect one's flock and practice an uncritical solidarity with one's own people. On the whole, the membership, and even the local leadership, is poorly educated in religious matters, and knows very little about theology and ethics. Religion is expressed predominantly ceremonially, emphasizing holidays, and a personal religiosity mingled with magic and superstition.

During the transition period from Communism to post-Communism, religious leadership acted out of weakness. During the Communist period—despite the greater liberality of Yugoslav Communists toward religion—institutional religion had been severely circumscribed and

---

4 STUART KAUFMAN, THE SYMBOLIC POLITICS OF ETHNIC WAR: ELITES, MASSES, AND ETHNIC VIOLENCE IN POST-COMMUNIST EUROPE, 244–45 (1998).

5 Based on the overview of *id.*, by ANNE-MARIE SMITH, ADVANCES IN UNDERSTANDING INTERNATIONAL PEACEMAKING, Vol. II, 1996–2000, 28–29 (2001).

6 *The Camouflaged Role of Religion in the War in Bosnia and Herzegovina, in* RELIGION AND THE WAR IN BOSNIA, 74–98 (Paul Mojzes ed., 1998).

religious leaders had been denied a public role. Later, when ethnic interests required a more pronounced profile for religion, the government and media started paying a lot of attention to religious leaders, especially the top leadership. Religious leaders, not having been used to such prominence and thinking that this would help their communities emerge from obscurity, allowed themselves to be manipulated by political leaders who sought "photo opportunities" with the clergy in order to gain popularity, a sort of religious stamp of approval. Only by about 1995 did religious leaders realize that the support they were giving to their respective political leaders was actually harming their religion. Many of them started distancing themselves from and even opposing, the regime. However, during the wars, religious leaders supported each their own side without any qualifications and a few of them became weapon-wielding extremists who demonized the enemy and divinized their nation and its mytho-history. Even now it is an ambiguous task to defend one's own people from the enemy and simultaneously promote peace. It would be helpful if some Balkan religious people would develop a prophetic voice and practice some self-criticism rather than merely direct their criticism toward the enemy.

The ways in which the major religious communities reinforced the conflict and at times stirred the passions and blessed the war efforts are many,[7] ranging from blessing troops and weapons for war to eulogizing political and military leaders of the war to condemning the "enemy." In the past this evoked anger and revulsion on my part, although I clearly recognized that even if these wars were religious—and they certainly were not primarily religious—they were fought by irreligious people. Even if the combatants used religious symbols, these were predominantly signs of heightened ethnic consciousness that was lightly draped with religious symbolism. A more recent insight of mine is that we ought not be surprised that the major religious communities contributed more to conflict than to peace. Religious people, like others, are generally a product of their own environment and the environment in which the religions evolved mandated that conflicts be resolved, regrettably, by means of violence. To most of them, this is the natural state of affairs. Power must be confronted by power or one must go under. Unfortunately, the NATO bombardment of Serbia over Kosovo reinforced this maxim in the minds of many. Religious leaders are unlikely to explicitly validate the formula "might makes right," but they do commit themselves to defend what seems right to them from the perspective of their own religion, even if one must use arms to prevent the destruction of their community.

---

[7] For a longer overview, *see* PAUL MOJZES, YUGOSLAVIAN INFERNO: ETHNORELIGIOUS WARFARE IN THE BALKANS, Ch. 7, 125–51 (1994). For a very extensive exploration by a variety of authors, *see* RELIGION AND WAR IN BOSNIA, *supra* note 6.

The hostilities of the various ethno-religious groups were so pervasive that they adopted the notion that, if you are not completely for us, you must be against us. I noticed in the response to my own writings and speeches that having tried to adopt an "objective," nonpartisan position, I was being perceived by all three sides as favoring their enemy. That was also the case with the United Nations, the European Community, NATO, and others of the "international community" who sought to be intermediaries seeking resolution by means of compromise. They were being perceived as "helping the enemy." Things got even more complicated when, for tactical political reasons, some members of the international community did start taking sides and began doing some demonizing of their own, as they did with President Slobadon Milosevic of Yugoslavia, the originator and leader of the Serbian war effort. As with the combatants, some of these processes of oversimplification and demonizing took place because they furthered the aims of particular countries or, as was true in the United States, of factions within the government.[8] But, whatever their rationale, they added to the bitterness felt by parties to the conflicts and made more difficult the task of achieving peace.

Religion's Contribution to Peace

In this task also religion played a role, but, alas, not a major one. Examples of religious contributions to peace are perhaps less numerous and visible, but they deserve to be mentioned, particularly since this was running so contrary to the contextual situation in which there were rather few peacemakers. For example:

a. Humanitarian and charitable services were provided by both domestic and international religious organizations. There were Catholic, Orthodox, Muslim, Jewish, and Protestant as well as ecumenical humanitarian agencies that relieved suffering not just to their own co-religionists but also to others in need.
b. Ecumenical and mono-religious prayer services for peace were held in many places, including those that had not been directly hit by the war.
c. An ecumenical journal, *Izazov mira* [The Challenge of Peace] was published in Zagreb by Serbian Orthodox, Roman Catholic, Muslim, Jewish, and Baptist editors.
d. Interreligious organizations were organized to work for peace and oppose the war. The first such was a grassroots organization named "*Zajedno*" [Together], organized in Sarajevo by a Franciscan, Marko

8 Insight gained at a conference organized in April 2001 by Harvard Divinity School on U.S. policies toward Bosnia, especially as communicated by James O'Brien, a member of the Clinton administration.

> Orsolic. Later an Interreligious Council consisting of the top leaders of the Muslim, Roman Catholic, Serbian Orthodox, and Jewish religions of Bosnia and Herzegovina was constituted. They worked for reconciliation in their country and for international assistance toward rebuilding of their shattered society. More recently similar initiatives for creation of interreligious cooperation have taken place in Kosovo and Macedonia.

Perhaps the most significant efforts for peace were made in the early years of the outbreak of the war by the heads of the major religious communities and other prominent leaders meeting together for the purpose of issuing urgent calls for cessation of hostilities and amelioration of suffering and pleas for the protection of religious objects, which were at times specific targets of destruction. Leaders participating in such meetings included figures such as: Patriarch Pavle of the Serbian Orthodox Church and Hamdija Jusufspahic (mufti of Belgrade) in 1991; in May and August 1991 and twice in 1992 Patriarch Pavle and Franjo Cardinal Kuharic, the Archbishop of Zagreb[9]; in Spring 1993 they met again, along with Jakub Selimoski, the Reis-Ul-Ulema; in May 1993 Patriarch Pavle and Cardinal Kuharic also met with Patriarch Sergius of Moscow (Mustafa Ceric, the Reis- Ul-Ulema decided to boycott the meeting until the Serbian Orthodox Church repents for its support of the Serbian war effort); in December 1993 the European Council of Churches sponsored a meeting of major religious leaders in Pecs (Hungary); and Pope John Paul II visited Sarajevo and later Zagreb. In June 2001 representatives of all major religious groups in Macedonia met near Geneva at the invitation of the World Council of Churches and European Council of Churches and signed a statement urging peace in Macedonia.

The texts of the joint declarations, when such were issued, were profoundly religious and peace-oriented but they did not receive a wide circulation domestically, where they had the potential for doing some good. Regretably, religious leaders domestically were more frequently defending their own nation's war activities than they were effectively supporting people regardless of their religion and ethnicity—other than issuing some vague statements that all lives are valuable and that suffering hurts all regardless of religion and ethnicity. Indeed, here, as in other countries, it is difficult for religious leaders to endorse a particular peace plan, lest they alienate those of their co-religionists who oppose it.

However, in addition to these religious leaders, there were a number of intellectuals, clergy and laity, who continued a level-headed yet

---

9 *Message of Patriarch Pavle and Cardinal Kuharic following their Meeting in Geneva on 23 September 1993, in* XII, No. 5 OCCASIONAL PAPERS ON RELIGION IN EASTERN EUROPE [current title, RELIGION IN EASTERN EUROPE] 50–52 (Oct. 1993). *See also* YUGOSLAVIAN INFERNO, *supra* note 7, at 147–49.

passionate analysis of the situation and dedicated themselves to peacemaking. There were clergy, such as Father Ivo Markovic, who has been honored as a *Peacemaker* by the Tanenbaum Center, to whom embattled forces on the ground turned when there was a need for negotiations or for guaranteeing safe passage. Additionally, both clergy and laity organized various conferences to help reconciliation, such as the one sponsored by David Little of the United States Institute of Peace in Budapest, in October 1997. Additional conferences took place in subsequent years, such as an interreligious Jewish-Christian-Muslim trialogue in Skopje in May of 2002. The actions of these individuals, those of foreign governments and those of international organizations to achieve peace, failed to end the carnage; in certain respects the war actually intensified.

THE ISSUE OF HUMANITARIAN MILITARY INTERVENTION

It is axiomatic that there are many situations when a war and related atrocities ought to motivate others who are capable of doing so to exert a greater force, including military force, to end the carnage. Everyone has seen situations on the micro and macro level when a stronger party seeks conquest and perhaps extinction of others and when more equally pitted enemies who began a conflict are unable to bring it to an end when it is clear that an outside agent is needed to break up and end the conflict.

This has both religious and political implications. Theologically speaking, we are often in the tragic situation that we sin either by waging war on others (the lesser evil) to bring an end to genocide or by remaining bystanders, doing nothing in the face of enormous evil. A sin of commission is not always greater than a sin of omission; one must weigh carefully which is the greater evil and which causes more guilt. Is allowing dictatorial regimes (like Milosevic's) or terrorists (like the Kosovo Liberation Army) or paramilitary organizations (like the *chetniks* or *ustashes*) to perform unthinkable carnage better than a military intervention by outsiders (war)? It would seem that evil is being caused in either case and that one ought to settle for the lesser evil (unless one is a situation ethicist who regards the "least evil" done lovingly to be the good).

That humanitarian military intervention ought to take place in order to prevent greater evil, in my mind, is beyond dispute. But there are a number of practical problems. One of them is that there are an overwhelming number of situations where such humanitarian intervention should take place—too many to be able to respond to all of them. Another is that it is rarely possible to foresee the development of a war—often it has a logic of its own in which it causes far more destruction than originally anticipated. Everyone knows that it is easier to begin a war than to extricate oneself from it. Might not the humanitarian action exacerbate the conflict into one marked by even more massive and long-term destruction? Who has the right to authorize it? (Any state can—or will—seek to justify any number of military actions on the ground that they were carried out for humanitarian purposes, but does this make it so?) Who has the power to effectively carry out intervention and will that state or organization be willing to utilize it? How much power should be used to effectively terminate a local conflict?

Those of us with some expertise and interest in the Yugoslavian situation followed with grave concern the deepening of the crisis in the late 1980s and early 1990s but most of us, like most people in Yugoslavia, discounted the possibility of war. Some thought if it comes to an engagement by the military it will be short and decisive—an error in judgment if there ever was one! War was certainly not inevitable. In retrospect, a number of better alternatives were possible including the almost never advanced scenario that to me seems much better than what actually happened, namely, a military and dictatorial takeover by a strongman (even one as vile as Milosevic) who would have later yielded to pressures for reform. Even a foreign intervention would have been better than what actually happened, but as we know, humanitarian interventions tend not to be preventive; it is only when we can no longer stand the carnage that we are moved to action.

What happened in the case of the disintegration of Yugoslavia, and especially the war in Bosnia, was that the international military intervention was too little and too late. The various international diplomatic, political, economic and other interventions were inadequate, as were the United Nations military peacekeepers at a time when there was no longer peace. To put it bluntly, though somewhat narrowly, the world cannot and must not allow a city like Sarajevo to be bombarded with impunity for four years while we keep watching it on our TV screens and finding that we lacked the will to intervene, because it was not crystal clear that our national interest was threatened. The loss of life was catastrophic, ethnic cleansing with all its grisly by-products was pervasive, the warring parties could neither win nor negotiate a cease-fire—all of this mandated a humanitarian military intervention long before the mortar shell killed many at a Sarajevo market and the Srebrnica massacre took place, which finally prompted us to act. It was a justified, right decision. Moreover, it was made by a legitimate authority: the UN Security Council.

A more serious criticism of the intervention in Bosnia and Herzegovina is that we decided to take sides (creating, for example, the Muslim-Croat federation, and seeming to ally ourselves with it) rather than simply telling all three sides to freeze their actions or else they will come to serious harm. Moreover, we failed to place Bosnia under a UN protectorate that would deethnicize the relationships. While I laud the Dayton agreement, it did have a bad by-product: it confirmed the ethnic structure of the government of Bosnia –Herzegovina—thereby creating a problem that has not yet been solved.

The lesson of the Bosnia experience is that humanitarian military intervention should preferably come before the massive loss of life. Moreover, it has to be sufficiently powerful to convince the local warring parties that they will be overwhelmed if they resist. I felt in 1993 and 1994 that the slogan "we do deserts, we don't do mountains" was the result of exaggerated caution and that the international community was capable of overpowering local warlords. A helpful factor in Bosnia vitiating against ultimate ethnic cleansing of any of the three nationalities was that they were in a rough equivalence in size. Hence a humanitarian intervention was not likely to bring about the elimination of any of the three groups and attempts could be made to work toward a pluralistic society sometime in the future.

On the surface it seemed that the lessons from Bosnia should be applied to Kosovo. That is what was done and how it was presented to the public. The argument was that the repression and killing of Albanians in Kosovo was too grave to be permitted, and that intervention could and should take place before the casualties mounted. Another argument was that the Western world could not tolerate a new Hitler in Europe—as if Slobodan Milosevic equaled Hitler in might. It was decided to wage an aerial war, which would minimize, if not exclude, casualties to the NATO powers and might be limited to the Serbian troops occupying Kosovo. On the surface it looked like a perfect example of justified humanitarian action and it was so lauded by many theologians and ethicists.[10] A number of American theologians wrote that it was a "just war" by the criteria of the classical just war theory (*e.g.*, Brian Hehir) while others said it may have been the first truly moral war that America waged, as there was no American self-interest in it. It was "Captain America" and the "League of Justice" fighting against malevolent forces to protect innocents.

There is, as is often the case, some merit to these arguments, but not enough to judge this war as either truly necessary or positive in the long run.[11] My view, to put it concisely, is that in the case of Bosnia and Herzegovina the humanitarian military intervention was good but in the case of Kosovo it was not.

For one thing, despite their geographic proximity, the situation in Kosovo was altogether different from that in Bosnia, in that it was not truly a multi-ethnic state nor one in which the inhabitants had had much experience in working together. Over the centuries Serbs and Albanians

---

[10] Otto Meyer, *Ja oder Nein zum NATO-Krieg gegen Jugoslawien—tertium non datur, in* 61 EVANGELISCHE THEOLOGIE No. 1, 81–85 (2001). Meyer presents the views of several Protestant (and Catholic) bishops and theologians in Germany, especially of Erhard Eppler, who, as a lay theologian, influenced greatly the SPD ruling party to approve Germany's participation in the war, despite constitutional strictures against it.

[11] *See* Paul Mojzes, *Faulty Logic, Faulty Ethics*, 116 CHRISTIAN CENTURY NO. 12, 406–08 (Apr. 14, 1999).

have alternated repressing each other, though there were also times when they lived alongside each other with little interaction. In the last quarter of the 20th century pressures from Albanian Kosovars had begun to spur Serbian emigration and the demographic ratio turned decisively negative for the Serbs, who by the 1980s made up only 10 rather than 50 percent of the population earlier im the century. Then Milosevic, who was actually the product of the Kosovo crisis, subjugated the Kosovo Albanians, trying to reverse the out-migration. After initial peaceful resistance by the Albanian population, an uprising took place in the form of terrorist activity by the Kosovo Liberation Army, which in turn increased official counterterrorism by the Milosevic regime and, ultimately, the massive repression and displacement of ethnic Albanians.

At first the international community applied various pressures upon Milosevic, with mixed results. By late winter 1999 the Clinton administration sharply increased the demands for international monitoring that led to an American ultimatum delivered at the "negotiations" at Ramboulliet. Had the Ramboulliet conference been conducted with a genuine aim to settle the Kosovo crisis, the war could have been averted; but the terms presented were impossible to any Yugoslav government, not just that of Milosevic. And when they were refused, NATO (though not the UN Security Council) authorized military intervention.

Several factors indicate that this decision was based on other than real humanitarian interests. President Clinton had survived the impeachment process two weeks earlier and welcomed a shift in attention by the public; there is nothing like a war to consolidate the public behind a president. At the same time it was NATO's 50th anniversary. Many had raised doubts about NATO's viability in the aftermath of the collapse of Communism and Russia's decline. Kosovo was an excellent opportunity to infuse a sense of purpose into NATO and strengthen American leadership of it. The credibility of NATO could be established in the face of those who might think it is a "paper tiger." Clinton's doctrine of humanitarian wars by NATO was born.

Otto Meyer, a German Protestant theologian, also argued that the strategic interests of the U.S. and European Community would be promoted in its eastward expansion. The recently conceptualized NATO strategic forces could be engaged, new military weapons could be tested, Russia could be put in its place as a second rate power, and a nonconformist state (like Yugoslavia) would be incapacitated.[12]

The problem with the military intervention in Kosovo was that the Clinton administration drew the wrong conclusions from the Bosnian experience. The thinking seems to have been (a) don't wait too long, (b) use overwhelming force, primarily by bombardment because that seems

---

12 Meyer, *supra* note 10, at 83.

to have been effective against the Republika Srpska, and (c) the Serbs and especially Milosevic had a sufficiently bad reputation that one could point the finger at them and say that they are the aggressors, conquerors, and what have you; thus, one could use strong arm tactics against Serbia and partition it, if necessary, and (d) use NATO rather than the UN to legitimize the intervention—a decision born in part of necessity, as there was no likelihood of obtaining approval from the United Nations Security Council.

The immediate reaction was that all hell broke loose in Kosovo. Instead of preventing ethnic cleansing, the aerial bombardment undertaken by NATO unleashed the ugliest period of killings and exiling of Albanians ever carried out by the Milosevic regime. In part, this was a reaction to the intervention, in part a reflection of a desire to "settle the problem" in a way favorable to Serbia.

It was, however, possible because the bombardment was comparatively ineffective against the Serbian troops in Kosovo, who dispersed, hid themselves and mingled with the largely Albanian population. Since NATO was reluctant to introduce ground troops into Kosovo, the forced exodus of Albanians continued until air strikes against targets in Serbia, which seem militarily unrelated to Kosovo, forced Milosevic to sue for an armistice.

While these air strikes were not directed against the civilian populations they were aimed at targets that had both military and civilian use, targets such as power plants, railroad and highway bridges, and communications centers. In the process civilians were killed. More importantly, the destruction of the civilian infrastructure had a deleterious long-term effect on the economy of Yugoslavia in general and of Serbia in particular.

Thus, while the intervention was successful to the degree that there was no loss of life to the intervening forces and that Kosovo was turned into a UN protectorate, the civilian population suffered greatly—and some would say unnecessarily—in the process.

One of NATO's mistakes was to regard the Serbs as bad guys and the Albanians as good guys. That mistake became evident upon the occupation of Kosovo by the "international community." Kosovar Albanians, those who returned and those who stayed, but mostly the KLA, carried out a more effective ethnic cleansing right under the "noses" of NATO troops. The number of Serbs dwindled to perhaps 1 or 2 percent of the population and the return of the refugees is even less successful than in Bosnia and Croatia, where the numbers are miniscule. In retrospect one wonders whether it was ethnic cleansing which was so objectionable to NATO, since NATO, the strongest military alliance the world ever knew, permits reverse ethnic cleansing to take place on its own watch. Well after the official ending of the war in Kosovo, the KLA continues to operate not only in Kosovo, but in neighboring Serbia and Macedonia. In consequence of this, it is difficult to envision the establishment of "pluralistic democracy" in Kosovo.

Finally, one must raise the issue of the long-range effects of the NATO "humanitarian" action. It has so undermined the power relations between ethnic groups in the Balkans that it is hard to see how it can be restored without additional wars, at great cost to future generations. The most damaging effect is the long-range encouragement of terrorist action by Albanian militants and extremists, who now set their eyes on either creating a "Greater Albania" or, failing that, an independent, enlarged Kosovo, as a second Albanian state. In less than two years (by February 2001) terrorist activity commenced in neighboring Macedonia, directly fomented by the KLA activists from Kosovo, bringing that nation to a state of low intensity war. And while that conflict has seemingly been contained, the long-run issue of the division of ethnic Albanians among three different political entities has yet to be resolved.

CONCLUSIONS

From the case of the former Yugoslavia one can arrive only at an ambiguous answer to questions about humanitarian wars. David Little has argued that the "just war" principles, developed by St. Augustine and other Christian theologians and carefully and thoughtfully amplified by Hugo Grotius, are a solid basis upon which to construct a modern doctrine of armed humanitarian intervention (AHI). I agree that the concept of the "just war" is, indeed, a viable principle at the beginning of the 21st century that can be amplified and refined for use in combating genocidal policies within sovereign states. However, while the "just war" criteria are sound, huge problems appear in their application to concrete historical situations. Here are some "red flags" that I see in regard to the application of the principles of AHI to the Kosovo situation, flags that should be flown when intervention elsewhere is considered.

One is that a military alliance like NATO cannot claim to be the "international community" and hence is probably not the *"legitimate authority"* which can authorize AHI. If NATO were to be judged as *"legitimate authority,"* what is to prevent any other alliance, one created, *e.g.*, by Islamic countries, or an alliance that Russia or China may make, from claiming in the future to also be the locus of *"legitimate authority?"* The UN, despite its limitations, is a better locus of decisions about humanitarian intervention.

Another has to do with the decision to intervene to quell violence within the borders of another state which is like opening Pandora's box. First of all, there is the problem of parity. Can one simply pick and chose where an AHI will take place? If, for instance, Kurds are to be protected by AHI, should it be only in Iraq or also in NATO's ally, Turkey? Does one dare to do an AHI in Chechnya or only in a small location like Serbia's Kosovo? Secondly, who is to define the nature of the conflict that justifies AHI? We all know that one group's war of liberation is often perceived by others as terrorist activity. If a legitimately elected government perceives that terrorism is affecting the security of the state, can such suppression of terrorism be condoned in one case and condemned in another? Why is it acceptable to wage AHI in Kosovo where fewer people had died as a result of Serbia's "war on terrorism" than in the case of New York and Washington on September 11, 2001? What should be the decisive measure? Is it merely the track record and how revolting and obstinate the leader of the country is, such as Slobodan Milosevic or Saddam Hussein?

The question of proportionality will often be an issue. When an AHI takes place, the initial decision may be for it to be proportionate to the results sought, but if the attacked entity does not succumb in due time and the damage becomes greater than the initial harm to the group at risk, does the armed intervention suddenly change from humanitarian to inhumane?

Conversely, if the nature of the intervention is not such as to protect the group at risk (as apparently was true in Kosovo) is it still warranted, or must its nature change in order for it to be deemed justifiable? In modern warfare one of the most difficult issues is the protection of noncombatants. What has been euphemistically called collateral damage often turns out to be heavy civilian damage. The debate as to whether many more Albanian Kosovars died after the beginning of NATO's bombardment of Serbia or whether the expulsions and killings were already intended by Milosevic's government before this bombing started could be very extensive, but we can be satisfied here with the understanding that even in AHI totally unintended catastrophic results may take place. And this is even more likely if those intervening give priority to extraneous concerns such as minimizing losses to their own forces rather than really concentrating on both the immediate and long-range needs of the people targeted for "ethnic cleansing." Under these circumstances an alleged AHI can turn into a war of aggression, particularly if the principle of "last resort" is not meticulously observed, as it apparently was not at Rambouillet.[13]

My overall concern is that the concept of AHI—as important and well intended as it may be—can relatively easily be misused to cover up wars of aggression not only by relatively malevolent governments but by

---

13 By the way, it is not my intention to say that there were no positive results from the Kosovo military intervention, but I regard the Bosnia and Herzegovina armed intervention as being predominantly humanitarian while this was not the case with Kosovo.

countries that envision themselves as good world citizens. David Little is right when he states that Rambouillet had the earmarks of "coercive diplomacy," rather than genuine negotiations and that this approach may have stemmed in part from a desire to barnish President Clinton's political image. Whatever the rationale, the result was to cause serious harm to Kosovo—and to Serbia.

One thing is clear: theologians and ethicists as well as politicians and diplomats will need to use all their skills in each concrete case to evaluate whether a particular war calls for a humanitarian military intervention or not. The first, halting steps in this direction have been undertaken. Progress toward agreed-upon principles will be more easily achieved than contextualizing them to each concrete, messy situation.

PART III

CONCLUSIONS

CHAPTER 10

FINDINGS FROM THE SEMINAR: A SUMMARY

J. I. Coffey and Charles T. Mathewes

INTRODUCTION

The purpose of this seminar was to evaluate the roles that religion, international law and force can play in preventing, limiting or resolving conflict, with particular reference to the practice of "armed humanitarian intervention," (AHI) by which we mean coercive action involving the use of armed force by one or more states in another state, without the consent of its authorities, and with the purpose of preventing widespread suffering or death among the inhabitants. Can religion endorse and/or restrain the use of force, and if so, how? What constraints on force are imposed by international law and how might these be further developed? What role can religion have in these developments and how can it best play that role? Are there dynamics inherent to the use of force which will affect the nature and the course of conflict and, if so, how can they be modified to bring it under control? When one shifts from constraining conflict to initiating it, as in armed humanitarian intervention, should the guiding principles and practices change?

These are enormously interesting questions about enormously interesting topics. The purpose of this concluding piece is simply to sketch the findings of the seminar, as well as to note the questions to which we have not yet found answers—and the questions that we still need to ask. In this way, we may program the completion of our task, even if it does not take place within these pages.

A. On Religion and Conflict

The first thing to note is the profound ambiguity of religious influences on violence. On the one hand, they inspire believers to preach and to promote peace. On the other hand, they contribute, through their teachings about war, to shaping the beliefs and the behavior of protagonists. And they have, as Professor Paul Mojzes pointed out, themselves sometimes been a cause of conflict.[1] This is true at least of the Abrahamic tradition, and we suspect it is close to an analytic truth regarding any system of belief all-encompassing enough to merit the title "religion."

This ambiguity can partially be attributed to a complex mix of archaism and modernity. The archaism stems from the fact that the religious laws governing war and behavior in time of war were written hundreds of years ago, at a time when the world was very different—and yet they are the law. Professor Sachedina, Rabbi Dr. Gopin, and Professor Johnson remind us that religious teachings are steeped in these traditions, which results in ongoing debates within the religions about how best to stay true to their origins while still meeting the demands of the present moment. Sometimes these debates result in definitions unfavorable to peace, as when some Jews equate the Palestinians with the Amalekites of Biblical times and in this way seek to justify their extirpation. Sometimes they lead to judgments that proponents of a given adaptation are, like those who justify terrorism and violence as legitimate instruments of *jihad* in today's world, on the wrong track.[2]

Despite this dichotomy, this seminar came up with manifold micro-accounts of the role of religion in contributing to, constraining, and ending violence. As Gopin points out, Judaism has been wary of developing a modern version of conflict theory but only because the necessary institutions needed to put such a theory into place are no longer existent. However, he also points out that there still are elements in Judaism that could contribute to conflict resolution, notably the law of "pikuah nefesh" which gives the highest priority to the saving of life. Shriver suggests that the tradition of just-war reasoning, which has found a real home in Christianity, may equally provide space to think about a parallel method of "just-peacemaking" which can provide public impetus and guidance for humanitarian intervention. And Sachedina argues for a return to the classical language of *jihad* rather than the distorted variant espoused by contemporary radical Islamists. Collectively, they remind us of the manifold ways in which at least the Abrahamic religious traditions can encourage peacemaking, before, during, and after episodes of "humanitarian intervention," however necessary they turn out to be.

In order to find a way to exploit the openings they offer us, we need to come to a new understanding of the role of religion in politics and international affairs in the future—somewhere between its prominent, if

---

1 Mojzes, Paul. "Religion and Armed Humanitarian Intervention in the Former Yugoslavia."

2 Sachedina, Abdulaziz. "From Defensive to Offensive Warfare: The Use and Abuse of Jihad in the Muslim World." See also Akbar S. Ahmed, "Ibn Khaldun's Understanding of Civilizations and the Dilemmas of Islam and the West Today," *The Middle East Journal*, Vol. 56, No. 1 (Winter 2002) p. 4, where he writes, "The killing of innocent civilians is specifically forbidden in the Quran, citing Suras 5, 32.

not dominant, position in prior millennia to its almost marginal influence in the past century. To do this, we suspect, we must ultimately find a history—a "usable past"—which understands that the modern political order (both the international state-system and the inner character of the "liberal political state" of modernity) is a response to the inter-ethnic and inter-religious conflicts of the 17th century. After the 20th century, the belief that the current order represents the best of all possible worlds is no longer as plausible as perhaps it once was. Wake up and smell the napalm: the 20th century has perhaps been the bloodiest century in history. It has also been the most irreligious.

This is not a demand that everybody "get religion" to become peaceful; indeed this position is opposed to all accounts which simplistically connect or contrast religion and violence. Religion and violence are neither identical nor opposites. If religious idealists have typically assumed the latter, modern political thinkers typically assume the former. But both are wrong. As all the authors included herein demonstrate, religion is too multivalent for such simplicities. But that is all the more reason to think deeply about the issue.

B. On the Law of Nations and Sovereignty

The inherent ambiguity of religions is not the only complexity that we have to confront in thinking about humanitarian intervention today. Fully as challenging is the hypothesized[3] decline in the sovereignty of nation-states, and the growing confusion (in which that perceived decline has a part) in thinking about national sovereignty in a rapidly globalizing world. The oft-repeated adage contains at least some truth: the nation-state is increasingly too large to resolve some of the problems it confronts, and too small to handle others. The growing recognition of this fact has led many thinkers, and some policymakers, to begin talking about living in a "post-Westphalian" world, in which the ideology of absolute state sovereignty—that ideology which licenses states in arrogating to themselves absolute and unchallengeable authority regarding what happens within their borders—is undermined by some forces.

These challenges stem from a variety of sources: a world-wide communications network, an interdependent world economy, a "globalization" of culture and, sad to say, an increase in intra-state violence which some governments are unable or unwilling to halt. For our purpose, the latter is the most important, as these conflicts are both flashpoints for more widely spread violence and manifestation of behavior which believ-

---

[3] I say "hypothesized" because the reality of this development is very highly contested today; but for our purposes the very possibility of it needs to be confronted, as it is part of the increasing difficulty in thinking clearly about the question of state sovereignty in the future.

ers, ethicists and political leaders alike condemn. Perhaps, as the plausibility of states' claims to such absolute sovereignty declines, an opportunity is opened up to make the bedrock of the international system something like the fundamental human rights and/or interests of the citizens of those nations.

This is obviously crucial to the future prospects for armed humanitarian intervention, and for humanitarian intervention of other sorts as well. If there is some way of legitimating international intervention into the "internal affairs" of another state—*and legitimating such intervention in ways which put real and solid constraints on the extent and character of such interventions themselves*—it should be seriously studied. We must not overlook the possibilities of the abuse of such an opportunity, of course; but the prospects for a "moral grammar of humanitarian intervention" merits careful attention. (In this context Ambassador James Goodby's proposal for developing a definition of "collective security," in which it is recognized that internal disturbances may threaten to disrupt not only other nearby states but the external state order itself, is a possibly promising line of inquiry.) In a world where the gap between rich and poor nations seems to be expanding, and the possibility of "state failure" seems to be increasing, any opportunity to legitimate missions to counteract man-made or natural disasters cannot be easily dismissed.

Unfortunately, all attempts to articulate such a moral grammar are challenged by the tangle of arguments that the religious traditions bring to the table. For the religious traditions are deeply complex and at least partially contradictory sources of energy and guidance. The differences among religions extend even to their views about the viability of international law and, especially, to provisos authorizing the use of force. Each of the Abrahamic traditions imagines the relation between religious and political authorities differently, due both to their divergent histories and to their different doctrinal claims. (For example, Jewish and Muslim texts do not express the same radical ambivalence about political power that the specifically Christian Scriptures of the New Testament, with their more "apocalyptic" tinge, seem to express.) Most important for our purposes, the religions differ with respect to justifications for humanitarian intervention, in ways that do not seem usefully to map onto religious differences, for the disagreements within the individual traditions are at least as sharp as the disagreements among them. These disagreements raise questions about everything from the contradictions between maintaining traditional sovereignty and securing human rights to the relative roles of religion and the state in this endeavor. Future exploration of the role of religions in international affairs will have to begin with the recognition that clarity is not immediately available, but may have to be constructed.

Furthermore, at some stage these attempts will have to grapple with the provisions safeguarding state sovereignty that are enshrined in international law, and specifically in the Charter of the United Nations. As said earlier, if these remain absolute then interventions, whether military or non-military, will remain erratic, whimsical and dependent on random factors such as the (selective) showing on TV of particular events. Yet not only weak states fearful of lowering a barrier to forced change but powerful ones concerned about a loss of sovereignty to institutions like the International Criminal Court will oppose general changes. Here, as in other fields, we may have to depend on case law rather than on alterations in statutes for legitimation of particular behaviors.

C. On Force and Conflict

Along with grappling with difficult challenges posed by the religions' complex and in some ways contradictory views regarding intervention, and the complexities of international law in motivating and shaping it, we have considered the important challenges to thinking posed by developments in the understanding on the role of force. How are we to relate strategy and ethics—are these necessarily opposed? Or are there ways in which force can serve in the difficult task of building a new, fairer and more peaceful international order?

The most interesting finding here seems to be the surprising, if partial, confluence of a pure "power politics" approach and a religiously-informed, "values-based" approach. The reason for this is simple, though often overlooked: humans negotiate the world by their values. Hobbes was wrong—and so are more recent proponents of quasi-Hobbesian theses such as Robert Kaplan.[4] As Albert Pierce argues, geopolitical and military strategy and ethics often "point in the same direction," that the fear of casualties is problematic both ethically and strategically, and since "most religious faiths have a universalistic streak to them," religious traditions are a powerful force for identifying with people quite distant—geographically and culturally—from us, in ways that can mobilize popular energies, and inform policy-making both directly and indirectly. For Pierce, religious communities and leaders have a major role to play in mobilizing popular support for international involvement, and for serving both directly in the policy-making process and indirectly in the deliberative life of public discussion to which such policy-making is finally responsible.

In more technical terms, James Goodby argues that contemporary international pressures towards developing a plausible program for humanitarian intervention may well require the United States to articulate a "Grand Strategy" which includes elements of devolution of responsibility, international concerts, and the delegation of tasks to subsidiary institutions. Furthermore, such a program will in all likelihood encourage

---

4 See his *Warrior Politics: Why We need a Pagan Ethic.* (2001).

(and rely upon) a developing understanding of "collective security" which can both guide particular episodes of humanitarian intervention in the short term and encourage the long-term development of richer international norms. Similarly, Andrew Goodpaster calls for the recognition of a broad and deep understanding of the meaning of "resolution" in the phrase "conflict resolution," to include "the building of social and political institutions to provide justice, law and order and human security."[5]

D. On Humanitarian Intervention in Theory and Practice

All of this becomes very complex when we look at the "hard cases" which collectively comprise the realities of international affairs. We were especially interested in moving, even if only slightly, beyond the shiny abstractions of theoretical discussion and attending to the concrete issues in a particular case. Hence our attention to the issues surrounding the international response to the crises which wracked the former Yugoslavian states in the 1990s.

Professor Paul Mojzes takes a hard look at the course of Western engagement in the Balkans in the 1990s and finds in it some important chastening lessons for advocates of humanitarian intervention. Most especially, Mojzes suggests that it is precisely those episodes that most warrant intervention—those involving truly horrific violence and murky positions by the opposing players, for example—in which it will be hardest to mobilize international will to engage. In particular Mojzes contrasts the "international community's" laggard response to the real crisis in Bosnia-Herzegovina with its over-eager involvement, spurred on in part by guilt at their dilatory response to the earlier crisis, in Kosovo; he observes that it is often where humanitarian intervention is most dangerous that it is most necessary, and where it is most easy that it becomes a way for the international community to reassure itself that it is acting "morally"—which all-too often means it is acting "self-righteously." Furthermore, Mojzes suggests that religion had a large role to play in inspiring the crises in the former Yugoslavia and in fueling their persistence, even if that role was sometimes hard to discern.

In contrast, Professor David Little offers a more encouraging picture of the deep logic that could stimulate the emergence of an international consensus on the propriety of humanitarian intervention. Little undertakes a rich analysis of the 17th century Dutch legal and political theorist Hugo Grotius, in order to demonstrate that the deep roots of humanitarian intervention stem from the same source as just-war theory writ large—namely, the need to find some way to constrain international

---

5 Goodpaster, "Religion, Law and the Role of Force: Operational Aspects."

actors in a situation where they seem to be fundamentally outside the canopy of any normative order. Just-war theory can be said to constrain action, while Little's development of it—a development which he sees as simply latent in Grotius's work and the work of his philosophical descendants—can be said to be a way of prescribing actions rather than proscribing them. (In this Little, Shriver and Pierce make common cause.) For Little, the complexities of the real applications of humanitarian intervention—complexities which Mojzes identifies—do not undermine the basic political and moral logic which encourages it; they simply demand that we exercise due care in applying the policy in the real world.

This is, however, an area where "political and moral logic" is the driving force, not religion. Despite the emphasis in all three Abrahamic faith traditions on acts of individual kindness by individuals, we have failed to find much in the way of positive guidance for, or impetus towards, armed humanitarian intervention. (In this respect, the document cited by Professor Shriver, *Peacemaking and the Call for International Intervention for Humanitarian Rescue* approved by the 210th General Assembly of the Presbyterian Church (USA), is a notable exception.) Whether churches accept AHI, as did the Presbyterian Church, or reject it, as did the Church of the Brethren,[6] we would all benefit from better understanding of their assumptions about the world, their views on AHI and their rationale for taking those views. In this, as in many other areas, informed efforts at building consensus is preferable to judgments reached in isolation.

II. WHAT WE HAVE LEFT UNDONE

There are a number of important issues which we have *not* addressed, both for want of opportunity and for want of expertise, and we should note these as well, before moving on to make some final comments concerning where we might go from here.

A. Questions Unanswered

First of all, we have only obliquely discussed one basic problem facing all attempts to develop a "pragmatically effective political ethic" out of the Abrahamic traditions, a problem noted by thinkers as diverse as Max Weber, Nietzsche, and St. Augustine—namely, the conflict between the Abrahamic traditions' tendency towards developing their ethic on the basis of "ideals" of justice and love, and the specialized, ambiguous and occasionally possibly all-too "realistic" emphasis on political life and military affairs which emerges in discussions on war and peace. Here we find in the Qur'an at least implicit sanction for harsh treatment of

6 "Nonviolence and Humanitarian Intervention." 1996 AC Statement, Church of the Brethren. www.brethren.org/ac/acstatements, 4/23/02

adversaries who are "disbelievers"[7] and in the Old Testament explicit instructions to "put to the sword all the men in it [a conquered city]" and to take as plunder the "women, children, the livestock and everything else in the city. . . ."[8]

Professor Sachedina and Rabbi Dr. Gopin, along with other commentators, have noted that these abjurations applied to another time and cannot be deemed operational today. However, this judgment highlights a basic methodological difficulty: how can the ancient, not to say antique, traditions of the Abrahamic faiths be made "relevant" to the modern world? To ask this is not in any way to assume the inevitability of, much less to endorse, a "pick and choose" scavenger's attitude to the historical sources; the developments in worldview, doctrine, and practice we seek to encourage in the traditions must be developments marked by integrity to be authentic. But it is precisely that insistence on integrity that makes the process of development so problematic. What modifications in "the word of God" are essential if they are to be applicable today and by what authority can they be made?

Another large question not answered is: What sorts of roles might religions have in working in the international arena, within international structures? (This actually will get us to the question of sovereignty, about which we will say something more below.) Are there tensions inherent in such operations, particularly for religions other than Christianity? There certainly are. Daniel Philpott's recent *Revolutions in Sovereignty* argues that the international order that we have inherited is, in significant ways, a reflection of Christianity (and more specifically still, *Protestant* Christianity).[9] What does this mean for people in other religious traditions—not only Islam and Judaism but Buddhism and Hinduism? What does it mean that they're operating within a framework which is perhaps not fundamentally neutral with respect to the issues important to religions, but is biased in some ways, more Protestant than Roman Catholic, more Christian than other religions? And how, given their fundamental differences in beliefs about freedom of religion, about social values and about religious activism, to name just a few, can the various religions agree on an approach to issues and if so, is this best done within or outside of the political superstructure?

B. Questions Unasked

Beyond the issues we have not touched upon, though we knew from the beginning that they were there, other issues emerged as important

[7] Qur'an 29:40 and 9:14, *quoted* in *Islam and Non-Muslims: A New Perspective*, 12 RENAISSANCE, No. 3, p. 10 (Mar. 2001).

[8] Deuteronomy 20:10–15, *quoted* in *Islam and Non-Muslims: A New Perspective, supra* note 7; at 21–22.

[9] DANIEL PHILPOTT, *Revolutions in Sovereignty: How Ideas Shaped Modern International Relations* (Princeton: 2001).

during our deliberations and seem to merit serious attention in the future. We identify here what may be the two most important.

One is that of defining—and obtaining agreement on—the rights that are essential to a "just peace." Obviously, different entities will have different views of what is required, stemming from their own socio-cultural perspectives and their own estimate of the causes of conflict; thus, the Carnegie Commission on Preventing Deadly Conflict concluded that only a wide range of political, social and economic rights could dampen the fires of violence,[10] a judgment echoed by Pope John Paul II in his call for full "social, economic and political rights." Others will argue that rights are defined and granted by ethno-cultural groups, not by overarching authorities; that some definitions of rights seem to reflect economic theory rather than either local circumstances or "natural law;" and that others may, at least in the short run, have such a disruptive effect on society that it is better not to insist on them.

This has two sets of consequences:

- It makes it difficult, if not impossible, to agree on the criteria for AHI, whether by individual states or by the United Nations;
- It sets pragmatists and idealists at odds over the remedies to be applied; will stopping the shooting in itself insure a long-term peace (obviously not), will limited remedial measures, such as equitable treatment by law enforcement officials accomplish this (probably not) or must reform extend to a desirable but probably unattainable end such as rooting out corruption (We hope not!).

Thus, *some* way of reconciling differing absolutes must be found if violence is to be curbed.

The second is the task of redefining international law so that is places on states responsibility for the conditions within their borders—or responsibility for accepting help when these conditions are manifestly beyond their control; without this there will be neither a basis for intervention nor criteria for judging what is a "good faith" effort at internal reform. Yet this is a move with tremendous implications. At minimum it will further erode the already declining authority of the post-Westphalian state; at an undesirable (and thankfully unattainable) maximum it could lead to the creation and enforcement of norms by a yet non-existent international authority. Hopefully, we can steer between the Scylla of doing nothing and the Charybdis of attempting everything and resolve issues one-by-one, beginning with the jurisdiction of the newly authorized International Court of Justice!

---

10 Carnegie Commission on Preventing Deadly Conflict, *Preventing Deadly Conflict*, (1997).

FIRST STEPS ON A JOURNEY OF A THOUSAND MILES

As with Mao Zedong sixty-odd years ago, we are starting on a long and difficult journey. Like him, we can visualize our ultimate destination; like him, we have no clear idea as to how we can reach it. That our destination is not a physical one but a conceptual one, the establishment of a more just and more peaceful world, makes it even more necessary that our first steps move us in the right direction. But unlike Mao, who was the head of a political movement and the leader of an army, we are outside the mainstream of political action, therefore the measures we propose must be appropriate to our status.

It seems to us that the first and most essential step is to recognize that different conflicts have different causes and that their resolution therefore requires different remedial measures. (To paraphrase a familiar statement, "if conflict has a hundred fathers, so must conflict resolution.") This means that we can at best identify and help to shape instruments that can aid in the prevention, amelioration and resolution of conflict, without claiming that they will, in every instance, achieve the desired result. Their application is a matter of judgment, with which reasonable men might disagree—and unreasonable men even more so. This is a matter of understanding, not of action.

The second step is to try to reach, across religions, cultures and polities, a definition of the rights whose violation might trigger political, economic and/or military intervention. This definition will necessarily be a compromise, which may not recognize women's rights nor the desirability of a "free" economy but cannot accept less than the safeguarding of *all* human beings from cruel and inhumane treatment by their fellows and/or from the dire consequences of natural calamities, insofar as these are remediable.

This is a task that can be undertaken by political analysts, like ourselves, as well as by government officials, by members of international organizations[11] and, above all, by religious leaders. Whether done functionally, regionally or by categories of organizations is in one sense irrelevant, as all must come together in an effort to reach a consensus—or at least a series of findings supportable by most participants—and tolerated by those who may not participate in the endeavor. (Personally, we would endorse a reprise of the study by the Carnegie Commission on the Prevention of Deadly Violence as a means of jump-starting an effort to define non-violable rights but, failing that, we may simply have to write more books!)

---

[11] The African Union has already begun the process by asserting the power "to intervene in member states in cases of genocide, war crimes, or gross violations of human rights. . . ." *The New York Times on the Web.* July 14, 2002. *Week in Review.* http://www.nytimes.com/2002/07/14/weekinreview

The third step, we think, is to start a similar effort to redefine the boundaries between the rights of states and the power of international organizations, boundaries which were set at the end of WW II and which have not changed substantially since then. We are not so naïve as to believe that this is something that can be done by study groups or commissions, but we do see possibilities in building on "case law," as spelled out in our Findings.

Last for now, but not least in terms of furthering our journey, is the effort to encourage—and where possible to support—those elements within the Abrahamic faith traditions that are seeking to "modernize" teachings about the role of force, elements such as the Conservative Jews, the Presbyterian Church of the United States and those Muslims who, while obeying the Qur'an and the Sunna, recognize that many of their abjurations regarding the treatment of nonbelievers have no place in today's world.[12] This is, as noted earlier, a difficult task, both because of the origins of and the ambiguity of some religious teachings and because of differences within the three faith traditions, as well as among them. It is also one where we cannot identify a *modus operandi*, which must come from within the churches. We do, however, agree with Karen Armstrong that this should not be a conflictual effort but a cooperative one, that "If fundamentalists must evolve a more compassionate assessment of their enemies in order to be true to their religious traditions, secularists must also be more faithful to the benevolence, tolerance and respect for humanity which characterizes modern culture at its best. . . ."[13] The one point on which we would insist, and this holds generally as well as in this particular enterprise, is that it must involve laity as well as clergy; otherwise it may be ineffective and our journey may never be completed.

---

12 "Islam and Non-Muslims: A New Perspective," *supra* note 7; at p. 8.

13 KAREN ARMSTRONG. THE BATTLE FOR GOD. 371 (2002).

INDEX